Words Beneath

Wings

Lauren Christine Frahn

MW01222437

Copyright © 2012
Lauren Christine Frahn

All rights reserved.

ISBN: 1477625305
ISBN-13: 9781477625309

Introduction

It was during a difficult point in my life that I found strength in reading inspirational quotes and at that point I decided to start writing a message to myself every morning. This message, along with my faith in God, helped give me the strength that I needed in order to get through each day. In applying my daily morning lessons to my life, I was able to get myself not only to a better place, but to the best place that I have ever been; I knew that there was a good reason for what I was going through. Similar to a caterpillar, I thought that my world was over, but it was at that point that I emerged into a butterfly...

My goal now is to be able to share them with you and to make a difference in all of your lives. I hope to be the "WORDS" beneath your "WINGS"...

Best wishes...and Butterfly kisses...
~LCF

"Be a "PILLAR" of STRENGTH during "CATERPILLAR MOMENTS" and BELIEVE like never before...
...that your FAITH will soon provide you with your beautiful "BUTTERFLY WINGS" to SOAR" (LCF)

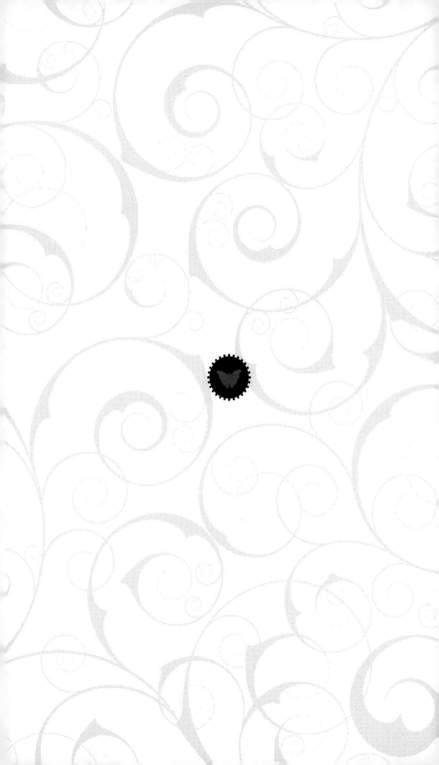

A-HA MOMENTS

♥ While it may be difficult to see the "silver lining" during a "RAINY DAY", the SUNSHINE will eventually reveal itself... "Golden" rays will eventually break through this "haze" ♥ Do not jump to a "foggy" conclusion, but wait for God's revealing "illusion". The quicker that you move toward this "light", the faster you will arrive at the "A-HA!" moment, where all "Answers – Have Appeared!" ♥ What you might be considering as a step BACKWARD might actually be the very event that will catapult you FORWARD... God's "GROUNDS" will propel you "leaps and bounds" and always put you on the "faster track" to SUCCESS ♥ When a "hard-SHIP" forces you to sail "choppy waters", relax and ride out the TROUBLESOME "tide", remembering Who it is that is "rocking your boat" ♥ Be careful that you do not mistake a MIRACLE for a "malady"...Do not seek "immunity", for God is showing you OPPORTUNITY. Find RELIEF from your GRIEF... Remember, God always has a REASON that will eventually bring you PLEASIN' ☺ ♥ (LCF)

Lauren Christine Frahn

ABLE vs. WILLING

♥ You are CAPABLE of attaining your GOALS, but are you WILLING to put in the required EFFORT? ♥ Just because you CAN, doesn't mean that you WILL... you must DECIDE for yourself to take the necessary ACTIONS in order to ACHIEVE GOOD FORTUNE ♥ Your CAPACITY for PROSPERITY is more than ADEQUATE, but your ENERGY must also be of the same CALIBER. There is an enormous difference between not being ABLE to make an effort and not being INCLINED or DESIROUS to do so...SUCCESS comes to the WILLING ♥ You are COMPETENT to be a "HEADLINER", but the CHOICE is yours as to whether you take CENTER STAGE. You are only prone to PROSPERITY when you don't play the part of "POWERLESS" ♥ (LCF)

ACCEPT COMPLIMENTS

♥ ACCEPT COMPLIMENTS instead of DISCREDITING them ♥ For whatever reason, it almost seems a tendency to REJECT another's PRAISE, but realize that it was given to you for a REASON...you DESERVE it! When someone DELIVERS you a message of MERIT, do your best not to "block the sender", for it isn't "SPAM" ☺ ♥ The next time someone speaks words in your FAVOR, do YOURSELF a favor and do not DISCOUNT it...simply say THANK YOU and feel GREAT! While you certainly don't want to rely on external APPRECIATION to determine YOUR internal level of SELF-SATISFACTION, it is okay to allow another's PRAISE to RAISE your PRIDE! APPROVE of "ACCOLADE" and be KEEN on your "KUDOS"! ♥ Do not "close the curtains" on the "rounds of applause" that are resounding due to YOUR performance...BOW and give an ENCORE! ♥ (LCF)

Lauren Christine Frahn

ACT, DON'T REACT

♥ Without the ability to TURN TIME in a "COUNTER-CLOCKWISE" direction, you don't get a chance to "take back" something that you said that you wish you hadn't. In the same way, you are unable to UNDO an action after it is ALREADY done. PAY ATTENTION to your thoughts and PLAN your actions, without MINDLESS "REactions" ♥ Always assume RESPONSIBILITY for everything that you SAY or DO and in doing so, you are also assuming responsibility for making your life the very BEST that it can be. Be sure that your next MOVE or WORD is one that will not cause REGRET and is one that FURTHERS your DEVELOPMENT and CHARACTER ♥ By ADVANCING your REPUTATION through your words and deeds, SUCCESS in your PURSUITS will become much easier..."ACT, Don't REact" ♥ (LCF)

"ADD-VENTURE" TO YOUR DREAMS

♥ Take your DREAMS into your OWN HANDS ♥ If you are WAITING on the action of someone else to bring you CLOSER to your desired GOAL, I offer you this...If it is something that ANOTHER can do, it is something that Y-O-U CAN DO for YOURSELF ♥ Take LESSONS from those who have SUCCEEDED on a SIMILAR path to yours and LEARN whatever it is that you need to in order to PROCEED...and get MOVING! ♥ EMPOWER yourself with the KNOWLEDGE that you CAN DO whatever it is that you set your mind to...When you RELY on your OWN abilities, you open up a world of POSSIBILITIES ♥ "ADD" your own EFFORTS to your desired "VENTURE" and EMBARK on the "ADD-VENTURE" to your DREAMS ♥ (LCF)

Lauren Christine Frahn

5

AIR YOUR FLAIR

♥ Never put a "CAP" on your "ABILITY", but "uncover" your "CAPABILITY"! ♥ You could possess ALL of the "TALENT" in the world, but if you do not APPLY it, it's tremendous VALUE becomes "worthless". If you don't have the "WILL" to make use of your "SKILL", than it's benefit is "NIL", so if you have "A WAY WITH" a certain EXPERTISE, do not "do away with it"! ♥ When God has an INTENTION for you with a particular "ART", pay ATTENTION to this "calling" that you will "hear" in your "heart"! Never take a "GIFT" for granted, nor SLACK in your "KNACK"...when provided with a "PROPENSITY", go after it with "QUICKNESS" and "INTENSITY"! ♥ If you were ENDOWED with a certain "KNOW-HOW", ALLOW this "FORTE" to be made known EVERY DAY! When you have "WHAT IT TAKES", "it" is up to you to "RAISE THE STAKES"...Use the "membership" to your "MASTER-SHIP" and "set sail" on the "sea" of your "SAVVY"! ♥ When you have the "CAPACITY" to make the heat of your "burning" DESIRES "sizzle", do not have the AUDACITY to allow them to "fizzle" ♥ "Showcasing" the "RIGHT STUFF" is ESSENTIAL to maximize your POTENTIAL..."Air" your "FLAIR"! ♥ (LCF)

ALONE DOES NOT EQUAL LONELINESS

♥ Do not be afraid to be "ALONE"...EMBRACE it! ♥ While it is a wonderful thing to be in a RELATIONSHIP, do not "relation-SHOP"...It is so important that you are not with someone just for the sake of BEING WITH someone. Look for your dream "DEPENDENCY", but don't be DEPENDANT on one ♥ It is unnecessary to RELY on ANOTHER to tell you ALL of the reasons that you are so SPECIAL when in fact, this type of "EXCHANGE" should be between you and Y-O-U! Use your "SOLITARY" moments to DISCOVER, or REdiscover, all of your amazing QUALITIES ♥ Find a way to be your own best "COMPANY" and take comfort IN yourself, BY YOURSELF. "FLY SOLO" and do things on your own that you normally would only do if you had a "CO-PILOT"...you will not only feel incredibly LIBERATED, but you will "SOAR" to new heights with the CONFIDENCE and STRENGTH that you gain in the process! ♥ Fill your "agenda" with the best "DATES" of your life...and hey, it's okay to be a little bit late...YOU are the only ONE that has to show up! ☺ ♥ Always remember that in the "equation" of EQUANIMITY, "ALONE" does NOT equal LONELINESS ♥ (LCF)

Lauren Christine Frahn

ARTIFICIAL SWEETNESS

♥ Do you only demonstrate "OPEN-HANDED" behavior with those who can place something in your "palm"?
♥ TRUE KINDNESS does not afford you the option of "picking and choosing" who you will be NICE to, based on who can provide YOU with the most benefit. It is far from NOBLE to have a CHIVALROUS attitude with "white knights", only to put on a metal SUIT of ARMOR with "minions" ♥ "Giving gifts" of GRACIOUSNESS with the sole expectation of receiving something in return simply means that you are "WRAPPED UP" IN YOURSELF ♥ The "sugar" of SELFLESSNESS will not mix with ARTIFICIAL "sweetness" or the "salt" of SELF-CENTEREDNESS ♥ The "reward" of GENUINE GOODNESS far exceeds any "award" that you hope for in creating FABRICATED COURTESY. An "ulterior motive" GENEROSITY "pales" in comparison to the LUMINOSITY that "shines" back into your life from "radiating" AUTHENTIC AFFECTION ♥ TERMS OF ENDEARMENT should not be "on your terms"... Fill the HEARTS of all with WARMTH and yours will "all-ways" feel the "heat" ♥ (LCF)

B.O.O.M.! (BELIEVE OUTRIGHT OPTIMISM MANIFESTS)

♥ Your THOUGHTS play a tremendous part in the DETERMINATION of how your day unfolds...it is so important to THINK and EXPECT all things GOOD and POSITIVE ♥ While this will require intentional EFFORT at first, the OUTCOME of your days will eventually make it EFFORT-LESS. Realize that every day is an OPPORTUNITY for you to DECLARE and DECIDE for yourself the most INCREDIBLE day possible! ♥ "LIGHT UP" your day intentionally with "BURSTS" of good ENERGY and "SPARKS" of only OPTIMISTIC VISIONS! Ultimately, this is exactly what will "REFLECT BACK" into your life! ♥ "IGNITE your day" like it is a "BOTTLE-ROCKET" by "lighting its match" with ILLUMINATING thoughts and create a day filled with SPECTACULAR "FIREWORKS"! Believe. Outright. Optimism. Manifests...."B.O.O.M"!! ♥ (LCF)

9

"BEAUTY-FULL" WITH THE "LIGHTS OUT"

♥ You may well be the most STUNNING person in the world to another...the question is, "what about if the LIGHTS WERE OUT?" PHYSICAL beauty does wonders for "catching one's EYE", but what are you doing to "capture their HEART"? ♥ It is very important to take care of your external APPEARANCE, for in doing so, you are nurturing one of your greatest blessings from God. HOWEVER, remember that it is NOT this beauty that "DEFINES YOU"...always be MORE beautiful on the INSIDE ♥ Do not RELY solely on your APPEARANCE to ALLURE another's interest, but rely on YOUR HEART to "capture" theirs. Sure, your physical ATTRACTIVENESS has the power to create a "parade" of thoughts "marching" through another's mind, but it is your KINDNESS and COMPASSION that will forever leave a FOOTPRINT on their HEART ♥ Be sure that your external looks can't "HOLD A CANDLE" to your INNER BEAUTY, for the "WINDS of time" may eventually "blow out" their FLAMES ♥ Even when it is too DARK to see, create a "BEAUTY-FULL" VISION by being the kind of BEAUTIFUL that RADIATES another's SOUL ♥ (LCF)

"DEVIATE from "the norm" and DISPLAY what makes you "DIFFERENT"! Being YOU is what makes you "BE-YOU-tiful"" (LCF)

BE-YOU-TIFUL

♥ We ALL have traits that we consider PECULIAR and that tend to be DISGUISED out of concern of another's interpretation of them. Do not keep these QUALITIES that you deem as UNUSUAL "under wraps" out of fear of what others may think. Understand that another's ESTIMATION does not determine YOUR VALUE...it is these "BIZARRE" behaviors and "CURIOUS" characteristics that make us each UNIQUE and ONE-OF-A-KIND. Act in the very way that you would if you felt that no one would ever pass judgment...ACCENTUATE YOUR "ECCENTRIC"! ♥ DEVIATE from "the norm" and DISPLAY what makes you "DIFFERENT"! Life is meant to be FUN...it would be silly NOT to SHOWCASE your "SILLINESS"! ♥ If you have "FUNNY" features, FEATURE them! Never change your "STRANGE"...Being YOU is what makes you "BE-YOU-tiful" ♥ (LCF)

BEG TO DIFFER

♥ Your ORIGINALITY determines your PERSONALITY. Never "compromise" your IDENTITY by "FORGING" another's SIGNATURE ♥ What makes you UNIQUE is what makes you "MAGNIFIQUE!"... Gain "POPULARITY" with your "SINGULARITY"! ♥ DEMONSTRATE these qualities that make you GREAT without feeling the need to IMPERSONATE! There is no reason to be a "CLONE" when you are AMAZING on your "OWN"! ♥ Attempting to make another's IMPRESSION your own is not very "impressive"... and is "regressive" to your personal DEVELOPMENT. To make a real "breakthrough", STAY TRUE to Y-O-U ♥ When you "PATTERN AFTER" another, you are creating a "HOLDING PATTERN" for yourself...You will never get AHEAD of the "competition" with REPETITION ♥ While it is okay to "FOLLOW SUIT" of another who is "wise", make sure that you are ultimately "wearing" your own "size". It is not easy trying to "FIT" into someone else's "SHOES", so CHOOSE to STAND FIRM in your own! ♥ Anyone can "PLAY A PART", but that means you are not "ACTING" from your HEART. "PRETENDING" to be someone YOU are NOT should never be a "goal", so always ASSUME the "role" that is

Lauren Christine Frahn

13

deep within YOUR "SOUL" ♥ Your VISION of SUCCESS will not become "clearer" if you are using "smoke and a mirror". APING another is "monkey business"...Do not make the "goof" of a SPOOF or the "gimmick" of a MIMIC! ♥ You were BORN AN "ORIGINAL" and not meant to be "copied"...Keep it that way, until the day that you can fit in a Xerox "paper tray"! ♥ In order to ADVANCE, you must take a CHANCE...on YOURSELF! If you are told that you must CONFORM in order to optimally PERFORM..."BEG TO DIFFER"! ♥ (LCF)

BOOMERANG ABUNDANCE!

♥ To ACQUIRE what you DESIRE, the concept that you must "grasp" is to first release your "un-FOR-GIVING" "clasp"...You "beGET" good fortune "FOR GIVING" ♥ In order to "TAKE IN" what you are "CRAVING", you must first "DELIVER" that which you "HUNGER" for. For a "HANDS ON" experience, you must first "HAND OUT" ♥ Do not be "PRIVY" to "DIVVY"...You are only doing yourself an "INEQUITY" by not DOLING OUT your "EQUITY". To "POCKET" MONEY, first "EMPTY" them out ♥ To do this "effectively, however, it must be "SELFLESSLY"..."DISPENSE" without "SUSPENSE" of any "RECOMPENSE" ♥ Do not 'FORGET' that if you GIVE only "FOR" the "GET", you will not RECEIVE. You must "loosen your grip", without any QUALM, before "opening your PALM". For TRUE GRATIFICATION, "HAND OVER" without "hesitation"...and with ZERO EXPECTATION ♥ This may go against what seems to "make SENSE" but, I encourage you to "GIVE" it a try...the REWARD is "IMMENSE". The greatest COMPENSATION for your CONSIDERATION will be your "sensation" of pure "ELATION" ♥ Live in "LUXURY" by FIRST opening your heart and helping others to do the same. Remember, that which you PROVIDE will come BACK to you "multiplied"..."BOOMERANG" ABUNDANCE! ♥ (LCF)

Lauren Christine Frahn

BUILD SUCCESS ON AN HONEST FOUNDATION

♥ No matter how BIG the STRUCTURE of your "achievement", if it is erected on a CROOKED foundation of FRAUD, eventually it will COLLAPSE ♥ BUILD your dreams with RIGHTEOUSNESS and RESPONSIBILITY if you want them to LAST, for in order to SUSTAIN SUCCESS, MORALITY is a must ♥ "Makeshift" schemes produce QUICK results, but they are also quick to FAIL. Using FALSEHOODS to further your progress is FUTILE, for lasting ACCOMPLISHMENT requires FAIRNESS and SINCERITY ♥ INTEGRITY is integral... if you want your dreams to remain UPRIGHT, act in a STAND-UP manner. Understand that in deceiving others, you are ultimately only CHEATING YOURSELF. "Success" built on DISHONESTY is a "house of cards"...it will always CRUMBLE when your cover is eventually BLOWN ♥ (LCF)

CALCULATED RISKS

♥ Going for your DREAMS is going to involve taking RISKS...make sure that they are CALCULATED ♥ You are going to be required to just "GO FOR IT" time and time again when pursuing your GOALS, but remember that your SOLUTION will come much easier when you use LOGIC...as in ARITHMETIC, you can't SOLVE any problem without first "doing the math" ♥ It is absolutely recommended to move SOONER than later when taking ACTION toward your DREAMS, but there is a major difference between being QUICK to respond and being RASH...Be HYPED-UP, not hasty...Be STRONG-WILLED, not headstrong...Be FIERY, not foolhardy ♥ Create the EQUATION for SUCCESS by ADDing ACTION and SUBTRACT-ing DISTRACTION...FACTOR in a well-thought-out FORMULA and MULTIPLY your results EXPONENTIALLY ♥ (LCF)

CALL A SPADE A SPADE!

♥ You best be BELIEVING that there is no prosperity in DECEIVING ♥ To achieve what you DESIRE, you must not be a "LIAR"...You will never move "HIGHER" if your "PANTS ARE ON FIRE"! ♥ Attempting to steer through life on SHADY "back roads" will eventually get you "lost" and filled with DESPAIR...Trying to take a "short-cut" with DECEPTION will ultimately steer you into the middle of "nowhere"! While "STRAIGHTFORWARD" may not always be the easiest "route" to take, being "DIRECT" is always the IDEAL choice to make ♥ DISHONESTY only "serves" as a DISSERVICE, for it is not only "DISTRACTIVE" from SUCCESS, but also highly "UNATTRACTIVE"...For incredible ZEAL and APPEAL, "honestly", "GET REAL"! ♥ A "KNOCK-OFF" is fractional in value to that of an AUTHENTIC...make sure that your words are GENUINE and of the high-est WORTH ♥ Always ADMIT to a mistake in order to "FREE" the mental "obsession" and "OWN UP" to a poor decision, despite not wanting it in your "pos-session"... Even if you made a choice that was "not so GREAT", only the TRUTH has the power to "LIBERATE"! When you "COME CLEAN" about a wrongdoing that has left a "STAIN" on your heart, you open the "right" windows of your soul for a "fresh" NEW START! ♥

Nothing is so "petite" that it would permit "DECEIT"... Even if a matter seems "itty-bitty", it still requires that you get down to the "NITTY-GRITTY"! There is no "hidden meaning" in the FACT that FRAUDULENCE is "demeaning"... Follow the ways of the WISE and never "disguise" the TRUTH with LIES! Avoid walking PERJURY'S "PLANK" by always being "FRANK" ♥ To be "TRUTH-LESS" is RUTHLESS...nothing "WORTHWHILE" ever comes from GUILE. Never hold a "RECEPTION" for DECEPTION, for there is nothing to "APPLAUD" when it comes to FRAUD ♥ For a "well-ROUNDED" life, you must take "care" to always be "FAIR AND SQUARE"! If you want "ACCOLADE", be able to "CALL A SPADE A SPADE"...and always be "liable" to be RELIABLE...NO EXCUSES! ♥ (LCF)

Lauren Christine Frahn

CALM YOUR QUALMS

♥ "FEAR" is merely a figment of your imagination... Stop thinking and start DOING ♥ Having "COLD FEET" does not mean DEFEAT...you must BELIEVE in your ability to ACHIEVE and at the same time, DOUBT your "DISTRESS" ♥ When the "plight" of "FRIGHT" enters your mind, you must FIGHT this "notion" with "MOTION"...The "tension" of "APPREHENSION" is released by the "satisfaction" of TAKING "ACTION" ♥ PANIC does not require "surgery", but simply an "OPERATION" of EFFORT...Have the DETERMINATION to WORK your way through "TIMIDITY" with the performance of "ACTIVITY" ♥ DISMAY is "DEMOLISHED" by becoming ACCOMPLISHED! ♥ Even if your thoughts create "WORRY", make MOVES in a "HURRY"...and "CALM your QUALMS" ♥ (LCF)

CARICATURE STATURE

♥ The true measures of your MORALE are your TRAITS and HABITS "behind the scenes". If they are not CONSISTENT with the STANDING "performances" that you give when "center stage", your "SPOT LIGHT" SPIRIT is not an accurate "GAUGE" ♥ Your positive "on camera" PERCEPTION should be one and the same with your "off the record" REALITY. Be sure that a reporter would have the SAME "article" to write about your OPEN-DOOR "press conference" as he/she would an EXCLUSIVE and CANDID "interview" ♥ The GENUINE "canvas" of your CHARACTER is worth much more than any "CARICATURE" that another "draws" of your "STATURE"...Do not be "ARTFUL" with your AURA ♥ (LCF)

CAST AWAY CLOUDS OF DOUBT

♥ There are moments when feelings of DOUBT may seem to "CLOUD" your VISION to your GOALS and DESIRES, but you must allow them to PASS through QUICKLY...Remind yourself that no matter what the "OVERCAST" thoughts are that attempt to "put a damper" on your "sunny" OUTLOOK, if this is your ultimate CALLING in life, you WILL find your way to the SUNLIGHT of your DREAMS ♥ Turn the "gray skies" of DOUBT back to bright "blue" by choosing to HOLD ON to your HOPE...when you do, this SKY is your ONLY LIMIT ♥ Be sure that this is only a brief "SUN SHOWER" by reminding yourself of ALL of the reasons why you deserve these very dreams of yours to be your REALITY...think of ALL of the AMAZING qualities that you possess that will help to bring them about...and RADIATE them from within ♥ OPEN UP your "umbrella" of CONFIDENCE and take shelter from the "rains" of DOUBT ♥ Remove any disbelief and get CLEAR, for the RAINBOW "after the storm" is about to APPEAR ♥ (LCF)

CASTLE IN THE AIR

♥ Take your IMAGINATION to the "brink", for you are CAPABLE of SO much more than you may "think" ♥ When building your "CASTLE in the air", make sure that it is way "above the clouds" - If you can already "see" this "DOMICILE", you must make your goal a bit more "worthwhile" ♥ You will GROW greater with each GOAL that you "realize" and with every MISSION that you "materialize", so make sure that your "MANSION" has room for "expansion". Never hit a permanent "plateau" when residing in this "CHATEAU" ♥ Keep your "armor" up against the "heated breath" of an opposing "spitfire" and never allow it to cause your "FORTRESS" to go "up in flames". Battle any "DRAG-ON" that serves as a "drag on" your desired DESTINATION, for you have ALL of the POWER to arrive at this "TOWER"! ♥ Let down the "DRAWBRIDGE" to your DREAMS...your "PALACE" of POSSIBILITIES is awaiting your ARRIVAL ♥ (LCF)

CATAPULT WITH CONFIDENCE!

♥ The first step toward your DREAMS requires that you take a huge "HOP" of HOPE..."CATAPULT" with CONFIDENCE! ♥ While it can be a scary "DESCENT", you must "assent" to take the "PLUNGE" and "expunge" any doubt! If you see a HURDLE ahead that is "insurmountable", remember that YOU are the one that is "responsible"! "DISASSEMBLE" what has caused this "tremble", for YOUR imagination is the only "carrier" of this "BARRIER"! ♥ TRUST that God will "brace" your "FALL" with the satisfactory "embrace" of VICTORY. Take a LEAP OF FAITH...knowing that you have a DIVINE "parachute" ♥Do not "SKIP" a beat in pursuing your "feat" or you will guarantee "defeat". Another will be sure to profit from your "fluctuation", so do not get "LEAP-FROGGED" out of "hesitation"! ♥ There are unlimited POSSIBILITIES as to what this "BOUNCE" will BRING, so speed up your strides and get ready to "SPRING"! Think only of the OPPORTUNITY that this PLUMMET "poses", knowing full-well that you will land on a "BED OF ROSES"♥ "DIVE" head-FIRST off your "cliff" of COMFORT in order to create "ever-LAST-ing" SUCCESS. Walk to the "EDGE" of what is ORDINARY... and "JUMP" to your EXTRAORDINARY!! ♥ (LCF)

Words Beneath Wings

24

CATERPILLAR MOMENTS

♥ Few things can "TRANSFORM" like the power of HOPE ♥ There can be times in life where it seems that you are merely "inching along", but it is in these very moments where you must decide to stay STRONG. Although you may feel like you are only "crawling by", TRUST that it is simply a matter of time before you can FLY ♥ If you ever feel DULL on the "inside", remember that this sensation will "subside"...Keep moving in STRIDE, for you are so close to the sensational "BRIGHT SIDE" ♥ When you feel "COCOONED" by darkness, do not "restrict" yourself with thoughts of DESPAIR...while it may currently be "concealed", there is an amazing process that will soon be "REVEALED". Do not permit "fear" to "interfere", nor let "trepidation" interrupt this "TRANSFORMATION", but hold on to PROMISE and allow this "METAMORPHOSIS" to carry you to your BLISS ♥ If you feel like you are "STUCK" with nowhere to go, be patient and wait for your calling's "LIGHT"... The BEAUTY of your purpose is soon to "EMERGE" and it is here that you will have the ability to "take FLIGHT" ♥ Be a "PILLAR" of STRENGTH during "CATERPILLAR MOMENTS" and BELIEVE like never before...that your FAITH will soon provide you with your beautiful "BUTTERFLY WINGS" to SOAR ♥ (LCF)

Lauren Christine Frahn

CHANGE STAYS THE SAME

♥ As ironic as it is, CHANGE is the only thing that stays the SAME in our lives ♥ Be sure that you EVOLVE with these "ADJUSTMENTS" as they come...Do not "resist" the "SHIFT" ♥ Even if you are a creature of habit, get IN the habit of making TRANSITIONS as life RECONDITIONS your circumstances...the circumstance of doing so will be making sure that you are always at the TOP of your game...Play the game of LIFE by making REVISIONS in your strategy AS our strategy, whenever necessary ♥ Understand that CHANGE is inevitable...As life RENOVATES, "innovate" your TRANSORMATIONS accordingly...ACCUSTOM yourself to CONVERSION and allow the VARIETY of life to bring out the very best "VERSION" of you ♥ START A "REVOLUTION" TODAY! ♥ (LCF)

"If your footsteps forward are taken in pursuing your true passion, than success will be your shadow."

Lauren Christine Frahn

CHOCK-FULL OF ABILITY

♥ Think BIG and dream BIGGER, making sure that your actions are "in proportion"...and you will manifest the BIGGEST of results ♥ You are GREAT, with a limitless FATE. You are "CHOCK-FULL" of WONDER-FULL ability. You have the HANDINESS to "reach" EXTENSIVE lengths in life. There is no reason to be "passive" when your TALENT is "MASSIVE" ♥ Do not "narrate" the FABLE that you are UNABLE because you have the CAPACITY to accomplish DREAMS that are "remark-ABLE"! Choose to live your life's FAIRY TALE...Never settle for a nearby "destination" when your DESTINY can carry you to a land "far, far, away" ♥ You will be "remiss" if you mistake yourself as "useless", for you will "miss" your ENORMOUS opportunity to ACHIEVE your "bliss". Do not develop a "knack" for "slack" when the ABILITY to "attack" GOALS that are HUMONGOUS lies "among us" ♥ There is no doubt as to what you DESERVE...which is EVERYTHING. If denial is "draining" your dreams, throw in the "stopper" and fill your "basin" with a "WHOPPER" of a plan that you are going to get to chasin'! ♥ Replace a "might be" attitude with the POWER of your MIGHT...Never opt for a "LIGHT LOAD" when you are CAPABLE of a "HEAVY-DUTY" ♥ If you "second-guess" your "first-rate" EXPERTNESS, you must "digress" from this direction of reasoning and "reconsider"...because you are CONSIDERABLE ♥ (LCF)

Words Beneath Wings

CLOUD #9

♥ It is not by chance that those who "PROVIDE" the most to others "COINCIDE" with the most "GRATIFIED" people on the planet ♥ There is a direct "parallel" between the BLESSINGS that you GIVE and the "BLISSFULNESS" that you LIVE. By always "OPENING DOORS" for others to live the BEST lives that they CAN, your "THRESHOLD" for THRILL increases again and again! ♥ Simply, the more that you DO to bring another "GLEE", the HAPPIER it is that YOU will be! You will never "HOLD BACK" your own "EXUBERANCE" when you manage to "UNLEASH" another's JUBILANCE! ♥ Adding "PEP" to another's "step" will "ELEVATE" you to "WALK ON AIR"...In causing another to feel #1, Y-O-U will float "ON CLOUD #9"! ♥ (LCF)

COMMIT TO YOUR RACE

♥ When starting in the MARATHON of your GOALS, DREAMS and SUCCESSES, take off with a "shotgun start", filled with VIGOR and ENTHUSIASM! Ultimately, however, this INITIAL ENERGY is not what will SUSTAIN you through the ENTIRE journey. It is your ENDURANCE when you start to get "short of breath" that will determine whether you ARRIVE at the FINISH LINE ♥ Sure, there are going to be times when the easier thing to do would be to "throw in your towel", but that is not how TROPHIES are WON, nor how MEDALS are AWARDED. I challenge you to keep in mind that it is YOUR DECISION to PERSIST that will ultimately change the entire "course" of your life... CHOOSE WISELY ♥ When the "RACE" gets a bit diffi-cult and you feel like looking for a "way out", remember WHY you DECIDED to "RUN this MARATHON" in the first place...and COMMIT TO YOUR RACE ♥ (LCF)

Words Beneath Wings

COMPARE YOURSELF TO Y-O-U

♥ There is no point in trying to OUTDO another person if in doing so, you are still "ON PAR" with what YOU have always done ♥ True GRATIFICATION and REWARD should not be attempted based on a "BAR" that another has set for THEMSELVES...it is a FUTILE attempt at ACHIEVEMENT, for really, you are not truly ADVANCING if you are not "RAISING YOUR OWN BAR" ♥ Hold yourself ACCOUNTABLE for your actions and make REAL PROGRESS by always IMPROVING a bit more than YOU did the day BEFORE...and REPEAT this each and EVERY day! ♥ There is no need to focus on anyone else but Y-O-U. There is no "maximum capacity" that you can reach at which point your SELF-IMPROVEMENT efforts stop being EFFECTIVE... the formation of the very BEST YOU is your "NEVER-ENDING" GOAL and "EVER-RISING" LIMIT ♥ (LCF)

Lauren Christine Frahn

COMPASS OF YOUR CONSCIENCE

♥ "GOOD or BAD", "RIGHT or WRONG"...Your MORAL "CODE" solves these "riddles" for you on a daily basis... Do you take "heed" of its LEAD or do you "mute" this INNER VOICE? ♥ "Silencing" your suggested SOLUTION is only a temporary "still", for its "whispers" of GUILT will soon remind you that you should have followed its WILL ♥ By relying on the WISDOM that you have WITHIN for GUIDANCE, you will be "steered" to the HIGHEST of STANDARDS...You are sure to go very FAR when you follow your ETHICAL "North Star" ♥ Trust the "INNER COMPASS" of your CONSCIENCE...it will always "point" you in the RIGHT DIRECTION! ♥ (LCF)

"CONSTRUCT" ANOTHER'S SELF-CONFIDENCE

♥ "CONSTRUCT" another's SELF-CONFIDENCE in themselves through your COMPLIMENTS and "BUILD UP" their INNER STRENGTH ♥ "RENOVATE" another's apprehensive ATTITUDE into one of FORTITUDE by taking the time to TOUT his or her TALENTS ♥ Move the "locale" of another's MORALE from SELF-DOUBT to CLOUT and "TRANSFORM" any self-imposed "restriction" into one of CONVICTION ♥ LIFT another's SPIRIT and "REFURBISH" their expectations on what they are CAPABLE of...ELATE and "RECREATE" ♥ "OVERHAUL" one's position from HESITANCE to HEADWAY. A "push" of your PRAISE could be the "nudge" that causes another to "budge". Provide the momentum that causes one's stationary "stance" to ADVANCE ♥ A sincere EXCHANGE holds the POWER to "CHANGE". Sometimes something as simple as a SMILE can cause another to "go the extra mile". No GESTURE is "too small" if it ENCOURAGES someone to GO FOR "their all"! ♥ (LCF)

Lauren Christine Frahn

CRACK YOUR OWN WHIP

♥ YOU know in your heart what DRIVES you and what is best for your overall WELL-BEING...it is only when you ACT in accordance with these BELIEFS that you will experience the most JOY. If you are allowing yourself to be "steered" in a different direction, it is time to remove this DETERRENT...and "UN-LEASH" your HAPPINESS ♥ If you are leading your life under someone else's "CONTROL", you are FAR from the PATH of life that will bring you the most SATISFACTION. "Break free" from this CONSTRAINT and "trot" to the "trail" of YOUR DESIRES as quickly as possible ♥ Do not "bind" your BLISS by allowing yourself to be "HARNESSED" by someone else's "REINS". When you allow **_your_** HEART to be the "reins" that GUIDE **_your_** ACTIONS, your HAPPINESS will be UNBRIDLED ♥ "Crack your OWN whip"...and "SADDLE UP" for the exhilarating "RIDE" of LIFE! ♥ (LCF)

Being "different" is how "ORDINARY" is transformed into "EXTRAORDINARY"

Lauren Christine Frahn

DARE TO BE DIFFERENT

♥ Being "different" is how "ORDINARY" is transformed into "EXTRAORDINARY" ♥ Make the CHOICE to answer your "calling" regardless of what others may say about the UNIQUE sound of your "VOICE"... REJOICE in your "RARENESS" with the "awareness" that this very "RARITY" is your key to amazing POSSIBILITY ♥ Do not allow others to "strike a chord" by deeming your melody "out of tune" or "absurd", for when their "monotonous musical" starts to sound, your "nonsensical note" will be the ONLY ONE that is "HEARD"! ♥ Despite having a "mission" that is "UNHEARD OF", "shout" your AMBITION "loud and proud"...Remember, the most SUCCESSFUL people in the world are those who SEPARATE from the "CROWD"! ♥ Any "ADVANCE" in this world is the result of someone taking a "CHANCE"...of deciding to never CONFORM...and DEVIATING from the "NORM" ♥ Create "ground-breaking" results by "BREAKING NEW GROUND". SUCCESS is sure to COME...as long as you march to the "beat" of your OWN drum! ♥ Realize that your "EDGE" is your "ADVANT-EDGE". Embrace what makes you DIFFERENT, for it is how YOU will MAKE a DIFFERENCE! When you act from a place that is INNOVATIONAL, you will create a future that is SENSATIONAL! ♥ For PROSPERITY that will "last", have the COURAGE to CONTRAST...DARE to be **DIFFERENT!** ♥ (LCF)

Words Beneath Wings

DECISION AFTERSHOCKS

♥ THINK THROUGH the "FOLLOW THROUGH"...Before taking ACTION, think about its CHAIN RE-ACTION ♥ CONSEQUENCES are not always immediate...Focusing only on the initial "tremors" of a SETTLEMENT does not take into account the eventual "AFTERSHOCKS" ♥ While it is easy to recognize the short-term RESULTS of every DECISION that is made, you should take a moment to consider whether your CHOICE is launching a "GRENADE"...Look "down the road" and be sure that you are not "igniting" a time bomb that will eventually EXPLODE! ♥ PAUSE...before you CARRY OUT a "CAUSE"...and think about the resulting FALLOUT EFFECT. Even if your SELECTION gets you off to a "sprinting" start, make sure that the OUTCOME is good for the "LONG RUN"! ♥ (LCF)

Lauren Christine Frahn

DEFERENCE FOR DIFFERENCE

♥   Within IRREGULARITIES lie tremendous OPPORTUNITIES... Look at DIFFERENCES in others with DEFERENCE ♥ REGARD another's DISCREPANCIES and have RESPECT for VARYING "tendencies"...For a life that is ONE-OF-A-KIND, you must keep an OPEN-MIND ♥ In reality, DISTINCTION prevents the "extinction" of INDIVIDUALITY. Look at VARIATION with VENERATION, for it enables the DIVERSIFICATION of our NATION...and with this DIVERGENCE comes competition's "EMERGENCE" ♥ Give ADORATON for DEVIATION, for it is one of the biggest catalysts for CREATION! If everything were UNIFORM, it would leave you with a small desire to learn and TRANSFORM ♥ There would be no GENIUS if everything were HOMOGENEOUS...It is only when something is NONCONFORMING that it holds the power for TRANSFORMING. Remember, it is usually an ODDITY that becomes one's biggest "commodity"... Use what is UNORTHODOX to help you "THINK OUTSIDE THE BOX"! ♥ There is no RARITY in SIMILARITY! To be EXCEPTIONAL requires that you first be the EXCEPTION...NO EXCEPTIONS! ♥ What you learn from one's PARTICULAR "trait" can be

the very KEY that "unlocks" the door to your ultimate "FATE"...EMBRACE one's "DEPARTURE" in order
to "leave" yourself with much to APPRECIATE ♥ Be
IMPARTIAL to realize your POTENTIAL... This very
RECOGNITION might be the key to your DREAM's
"ignition" ♥ (LCF)

DESIGN THE REALITY OF YOUR DAYDREAMS

♥ That thing that you daydream about? That VISION that ELEVATES your spirits and carries your soul to the land of BLISS? Imagine how AMAZING you would feel if that could be YOUR reality each and every day! Picture the EXCITEMENT that would propel you out of bed each and every morning knowing that you are starting another day in your DREAM world! ♥ FEEL the complete sense of JOY and HAPPINESS that would envelop your heart living the life that you would create for yourself if you in fact had the ability to DESIGN your own REALITY! Well, guess what? ...You DO...and you CAN!! ♥ (LCF)

DESIGNATE YOUR FATE

♥ FREEDOM enables us the OPPORTUNITY to make our OWN WAY...What will you do with your LEEWAY today? "OPT FOR" ADVANCEMENT ♥ Every "ELECTION" will determine your path's "DIRECTION". Put yourself to the "test" of LIFE...Be SELECTIVE with your ELECTIVES knowing that every DECISION "counts" toward your ultimate "grade" ♥ "APPOINT" with a "PURPOSE-FULL" point, so as not to "DISAPPOINT", nor subtract from your overall PURPOSE ♥ "SIFT OUT" the options that do not serve you in order to "REFINE" the PROGRESS toward your ultimate GOALS. When a "SELECTION" will bring you more feelings of DOUBT than CLOUT..."OPT OUT"! ♥ The only way you can "lose" is if you don't make the most of your ABILITY to "CHOOSE"..."SELECT" with SENSIBILITY for unlimited POSSIBILITY! ♥ "DESIGNATE" your FATE to be nothing less than GREAT! Do not "SETTLE UPON" a "makeshift" scheme, but DECIDE to "shift" into high gear toward every HOPE and DREAM! CHALLENGE yourself with your "CHOICES"! ♥ "MAKE UP YOUR MIND" to CHOOSE a future that is SUBLIME...One DECISION at a time ♥ (LCF)

Lauren Christine Frahn

41

DIS-APPEARANCE

♥ A BEAUTIFUL FACE does not compensate for an ATTITUDE of DISGRACE ♥ Never be under the "supposition" that BEAUTY can "mask" DEFECTS in DISPOSITION. No matter how PRESENTABLE your APPEARANCE, you can guarantee its "DIS-APPEARANCE" if your personality is RESENTABLE! ♥ The clearest of COMPLEXIONS will seem covered with IMPERFECTIONS if your CHARACTER "FLAWS" cast off "UNSIGHTLY" REFLECTIONS. The most stunning of FIGURES will lose its "shape" if your "frame of mind" is UNKIND! "Even" the most FLAWLESS of skin will appear BLEMISHED if you are "discolored" WITHIN ♥ No matter how ATTRACTIVE your ALLURE, an UNFRIENDLY demeanor is DETRACTIVE, for sure! You can be outwardly ADORABLE, but instantly become not so "cute" if you are inwardly DEPLORABLE ♥ If your MOOD is RUDE, even LOOKS worthy of "accolade" are sure to quickly FADE. You can be extremely BECOMING, but that will not stop you from "becoming" UNAPPEALING if you "display" no kindness or warm FEELING. A DAZZLING "disguise" can never "rationalize" an AURA of deceitfulness and lies, nor is there a FEATURE that can holds its CHARM against a temper that causes another HARM ♥ There is no VARNISH that can cover the "TARNISH" of a DULL "UNDERTONE"...If you want to maintain your RADIANT "SHINE", make sure that your INNER "GLOW" is equally DIVINE! ♥ (LCF)

DIVINELY STEERED

♥ Do you just RELY on God when you are WISHING for something or do you allow your FAITH to GUIDE you? ♥ When you put your TRUST in God that He will LEAD you down whatever "road" is BEST, as only He KNOWS, it makes it easier to RELAX. Nothing is accomplished without MAKING MOVES toward your GOALS, but allow them to be "INSPIRED ACTIONS" ♥ You will know when you are being "DIVINELY STEERED" because this MOTIVATION and IMPULSE will "grab a hold" of your HEART and not let go, no matter how many times you try to "step on the break" or "turn the wheel" in a different DIRECTION ♥ Stop trying to CONTROL everything and allow your PRAYER and FAITH in GOD to be your "cruise control". Allowing God to "fasten your seat belt" is the sure way to "SECURE" your HAPPINESS ♥ Keep your eyes straight and get READY for your "GREEN LIGHT" to "hit the gas". Stop trying to follow your own "road map"...You will ACHIEVE whatever God has in store for you when you and allow HIM to NAVIGATE you ♥ (LCF)

DOES YOUR "MAKEUP" WASH OFF?

♥ Your "colorful" REPUTATION does not mean much if the QUALITY of your DISPOSITION "pales" in comparison. It is the INTEGRITY of the TONE that you demonstrate when ALONE that far exceeds the HUE that you "assume" only when in another's VIEW ♥ Whether your BEHAVIOR is consistently RIGHTEOUS, only you will know...just remember that simply because others may THINK it "GREAT", doesn't make it so! In order to be a really good person, you REALLY have to BE a good person! Make sure that your "social" STYLE matches your "at-home" ATTRIBUTES ♥ Is the MAKEUP of your PERSONALITY only "seen in public", or is it a "COVER-UP" that "washes off" in private? Do not create a FALSE "ILLUSION" with a BEAUTIFUL "MASK" if you REMOVE it "BEHIND CLOSED DOORS" ♥ (LCF)

Lauren Christine Frahn

DO NOT "SPEED-READ" THROUGH LIFE

♥ A BOOK is much more ENJOYABLE when you actually READ the WORDS on the pages, right? ☺ While "SPEED-READING" accomplishes getting you from the front of the book to the back cover, much of what is COVERED is not DISCOVERED...the intended MESSAGE and most of the DETAILS are LOST along the way. Well, the very same is true of LIFE ♥ Thoughtlessly RUSHING through life does not give you much to think about ♥ Everything has already been put on the timelines of our lives in its intended (and PROPER) order...be ENGAGED in the process, ENJOY the steps along the way...and RELAX. God has authored our BIOGRAPHIES and does not require our attempts at co-authoring or trying to "hurry" His PERFECTION ♥ Our stories are ALREADY WRITTEN...trying to RUSH through the process doesn't make our DESTINY occur any quicker...it just causes us to MISS A LOT along the way♥ When you take the time to enjoy EVERY "page" of your life's STORY, you will GAIN so much more from the EXPERIENCE. It is FASCINATING to get lost in a good mystery book, but there is no greater mystery to be fully ENGROSSED in than the one that goes by the title of "YOUR LIFE" ♥ With PATIENCE, comes REWARD ♥ (LCF)

Words Beneath Wings

DOWN-TO-EARTH

♥ While nothing is IMPOSSIBLE, make sure that your ambitions are PROBABLE ♥ Strive to achieve UNREAL results, but be RATIONAL in your attempts... There is NO SENSE in competing with a goal that is SELF-DEFEATING ♥ Be SENSIBLE when "setting your bar", so as not to raise it to NONSENSICAL "heights". There is no reason to not be REASONABLE in your objectives ♥ Set your "SIGHTS" on the STARS without being "STARRY-EYED"...Make your FANTASY your REALITY, but do not "live" in a "FANTASY WORLD" ♥ Stay "LEVEL-headed" with your intentions in order to "tip the scales" of accomplishing them in your favor ♥ Plan for an END RESULT that is not only ACHIEVABLE, but also BELIEVABLE, in order to have ZERO DOUBTS that your "PROJECT-ile" will hit its "GROUND ZERO" destination! ♥ Set your TARGET at a range that is "APPLICABLE" so that the thought of hitting this "BULLS-EYE" is not "DESPICABLE" ♥ Go after your dreams with ZEAL, but be sure to "stay REAL"...You can be TACTICAL without being IMPRACTICAL. As a "MATTER-OF-FACT", for a mission to be remarkable, it must first be WORKABLE ♥ For your goals to bring the "COMMON SENSEs" of ACCOMPLISHMENT and MIRTH, always remember to "REACH FOR THE MOON", but stay "DOWN-TO-EARTH"! ♥ (LCF)

Lauren Christine Frahn

DREAM HOME

♥ The ASPIRATION that "DWELLS" within you is there for a REASON...It has specifically chosen your HEART as its perfect LOCATION ♥ If there is a thought in your HEAD that you are not capable of providing this HOPE a good HOMESTEAD, "evict" it and "move in" CONFIDENCE, INSTEAD! There is not enough "ROOM" for RELUCTANCE with the "DENIZEN" of your DREAMS! ♥ Remember, as opposed to this lack of "SPACE" for UNCERTAINTY, when it comes to the Universe's SUPPLY to meet the DEMANDS of your GOALS, it is UNLIMITED...and so is your POTENTIAL! Not everyone wants the same "FURNISHINGS" or the same piece of "PROPERTY"...With the world's population "possessing" different DESIRES, it is impossible for the universe to "run out" of whatever it is that you WISH for! ANYTHING and EVERYTHING is possible for Y-O-U ♥ Do not "HOUSE" any DOUBT that when it comes to your DREAMS, there is "NO PLACE LIKE HOME" to "raise them". Whatever the ENTERPRISE that "RESIDES" within, it is up to YOU to make it COME TRUE ♥ (LCF)

DREAM TEAM

♥ FELLOWSHIPS are meant to "LIGHT your FIRE", so be sure that your "TURNOUT" does not cause you to "burn-out". "CHARGE your BATTERY" with POSITIVE energy PROPONENTS and avoid any "components" that might serve as a "DRAIN" ♥ Beware of those that "pick" at you...They will slowly pull off the "bandage" that "glues" you to your GOALS..."Stick" only with the "gauze" that is GAINFUL and remove the "casts" that are determined to be PAINFUL ♥ Take an ANTAGONIST "antitoxin" by keeping your surroundings "germ-free"...and counter-act any effects of "poisonous" INTERACTIONS. Write your own "prescription" for POSITIVITY by getting your daily doses of "healthful" HELPERS...the assemblage of a "wholesome" BODY is "just what the doctor would have ordered" ♥ Your AGGREGATION should not "work up" AGGRAVATION, but rather endorse you in your CAREER. Assemble a SYNDICATE of those who ADVOCATE you and congregate with a CLAN that supports your ulti-mate PLAN. Those that you MUSTER should not cause you to "fluster"...In your "inventory" of BACKERS, do not "stockpile" any SLACKERS ♥ BUILD your "DREAM TEAM" with "constructive" COMPANY and make your SUPPORTS the most "upright" of COHORTS...Use only the strongest of PILLARS, so as to become a "TOWER OF STRENGTH" ♥ (LCF)

Lauren Christine Frahn

49

ESCAPE THE HANDCUFFS
OF INACTION

♥ While the world is MAGICAL in so many ways, your DREAMS do not just "APPEAR" out of "thin air"...The only useful "TRICKERY" or "WIZARDRY" is that of ACTIVITY ♥ An attitude of "I CAN'T" is just as effective as an "ABRA-CADABRA" chant. There is no "VOO-DOO" for ACCOMPLISHING your ASPIRATIONS unless "YOU-DO" the necessary steps on your "TO-DO" list! ♥ You will not "reach" SUCCESS by pulling a "RABBIT out of a hat"...the only way to make the "jump" to your GOALS is to have a lot of productive tasks "in the HOPPER". Jumping through "HOOPS of fire" is an aimless "objective" ...Performing a "HOOPLA" of ACTION should be your only "PERSPECTIVE" ♥ In order to ACHIEVE, you must "VANISH" from the land of "MAKE-BELIEVE". Replace "SORCERY" with EFFICACY...and "ESCAPE" the "HANDCUFFS" of INACTION ♥ (LCF)

EVERYDAY HOLIDAY

♥ The CELEBRATORY SPIRIT is not one that should be reserved for a few "OCCASIONS" throughout the YEAR, but rather a DAILY decision made by all to spread HAPPINESS, WELL-BEING and CHEER ♥ "RESOLVE" to make every moment "count" and do not "drop" the "ball", for new OPPORTUNITY exists day in and day out to PROSPER and give LIFE your "all" ♥ Make LOVE and AFFECTION a "routine" goal by "greeting" each morning with a "HUG" and a "KISS"...Touch the HEARTS of others whenever you can and develop your "relationship" with total BLISS ♥ Come across your LUCKY "four-leaf clover" by wishing others GOOD FORTUNE "over-and-over" ♥ Do not "PASS OVER" an opportunity to make "some-bunny" "HOPPY" and GLAD, for every day that the sun "HAS RISEN" provides us the CHOICE to "REJOICE" ♥ Set the souls of others on "FIRE" with your ability to INSPIRE...and use your FREEDOM to demonstrate wonderful "WORKS" ♥ Never "TRICK" others with a scary "COSTUME" over your true colors...your inside "SWEETNESS" is a TREAT that should always REPEAT ♥ You RECEIVE even more when you GIVE, so always say "THANKS" when

Lauren Christine Frahn

"GIVING"...To "harvest" an abundance of GRATITUDE is such an amazing way to be LIVING ♥ The feeling of JOY in your soul will "abound" when you choose to GIFT to others "year-round" , so "DECK THE HALLS" of each day with "boughs of holly"...and be JOLLY ♥ It is not necessary to have a "HOLY DAY" in order to make your day a "HOLIDAY"...Regardless of the SEASON or REASON, "FESTIVITY" should be an "all-year" ACTIVITY ♥ (LCF)

EVERYDAY OPPORTUNITY

♥ Here's to NEW BEGINNINGS ♥ There is a common "school" of thought that RESOLUTIONS are to be reserved for the "first day" of the year. If you are a "student" in that "study group", it is time to move to the "head of the class"...LEARN the LESSONS, "raise your hand", and PARTICIPATE on a daily basis ♥ While it is true that "C's" do "get degrees", do not settle for the lower "mark", but MAKE YOUR MARK... and go for the "A+" ♥ When you RAISE your expectations for what you can ACHIEVE and do the necessary "homework", you will undoubtedly GRADUATE to the HIGHER levels of your DREAMS ♥ Keep your eyes on your "own paper"...only YOU have the correct ANSWERS to the "essay questions" about your personal HAPPINESS and SUCCESS ♥ OPEN up the "books" of OPPORTUNITY and embrace every "page". Every day provides us the OPPORTUNITY for a FRESH start and a "clean slate" to "chalk up" with ACTIONS that FULFILL our deepest DREAMS and DESIRES ♥ Be sure that your "foreword" is filled with HOPE and LIMITLESS POTENTIAL. Make certain that every "series" is more exciting than the last, so that the final CHAPTER is a "HAPPILY EVER AFTER"... The End ;) ♥ (LCF)

Lauren Christine Frahn

EVERYONE CAN DO SOMETHING

♥ Never "turn your back" on one who has a "LACK". Ignoring someone who could use your AID does not cause it to "FADE" away...the only thing that "PALES" is your effort ♥ EVERYONE can give SOMETHING...DO or DONATE what you CAN ♥ By GIVING to "CHARITY", you GAIN the "CLARITY" of the tremendous impact even the slightest amount of your "TENDER" can "RENDER". Keep in mind that what you PROVIDE does not have to be of monetary value...you cannot put a "price tag" on the VALUE of SERVICE. Do not "PRETEND" to be of PASSIVE nature, for when you "EXTEND" a helping hand, the impact you have is MASSIVE ♥ There are NO EXCUSES for NOT doing a good DEED for someone "in NEED"...No matter how "LITTLE" you may deem the gesture, the results for another's well-being will be "GIANT"! Remember, it is not essential to HAVE a "great deal" in order to MAKE a GREAT DEAL of DIFFERENCE! ♥ (LCF)

EXCUSES OR RESULTS...YOU DECIDE

♥ RESULTS and EXCUSES are "MUTUALLY EXCLUSIVE"... YOU DECIDE ♥ Which ONE are you going to CHOOSE? Well, that depends on whether you like to "WIN" or to "LOSE"! When it comes to ACHIEVEMENT, or lack thereof, are you going to come up with an EXPLANATION or be the next great SENSATION? ♥ You can EITHER come up with a "SONG AND DANCE" OR you can decide once-and-for-all to TAKE A CHANCE! Step out of your "COVER-UP" and put on your "makeup"... tear up your "COVER STORY'S" page and take "center stage!" ♥ Do not come up with a "MAKESHIFT reason" as to why you are going to "sit out" this SEASON, but "MAKE the SHIFT" to "suit up" in FULL GEAR while you are HERE!! While a "DEFENSE" can win a GAME, if you create one for the "game" of LIFE, you are the only one to BLAME! There is absolutely no "JIVE" as to why you do not STRIVE to make the very most of being ALIVE! ♥ "Reveal" your DETERMINATION by not fooling yourself with an EXPLANATION for your advancement's "EVASION"...You cannot DIS"COVER" your POTENTIAL if you stay "hidden" underneath a "COVER"! Do not "sink" yourself with a "FISH STORY" as to why you do not "cast your rod" to "hook" your

Lauren Christine Frahn

ultimate "GLORY"! ♥ Remember, there is absolutely no COMPATIBILITY between "ALIBI" and "ABILITY", nor are there any "GROUNDS" as to why your GOALS do not "GROW in leaps and BOUNDS"! ♥ You have EVERY good "REASON" as to WHY you should TRY to REACH FOR every STAR in the "SKY"...there is just no RATIONALIZATION for STAGNATION ♥ If you want to be SUCCESSFUL at your life "CALLING", you must first quit your "STALLING"!...ACCOMPLISHMENT cannot CO-EXIST with "COP-OUTS"♥ (LCF)

EXTRA "OOMPH"!

♥ Get FARTHER by giving FURTHER...An "OVERFLOW" of EFFORT brings a "SURPLUS" of SUCCESS ♥ Even in the most routine of tasks, DO MORE than what is asked! Give the "OLD COLLEGE TRY" every day with any endeavor that is "UNDERway"...and graduate at the "TOP" of your class! ♥ When you AIM for the HIGHEST "MARK", you can never truly "fail"...Why just get an ""A" FOR EFFORT" when there is an A+ on the "scale"? ♥ When you have met a REQUIREMENT, do not allow for your "retirement". In order to stay "AHEAD" of the competition, you must keep "OUT OF REACH" ♥ Go the "EXTRA MILE" so that you can look back at your ACHIEVEMENT with a SMILE...and hey, take one more step for "good measure" to ADD even MORE to this PERFORMANCE "pleasure"! ♥ Always give the extra "OOMPH!"... "_O_utdo, _O_utperform & _M_ake _P_rosperity _H_appen!" ♥ Another's "MAXIMUM" should be your point of "MOMENTUM" ♥ WORLD RECORDS are the result of someone BELIEVING that they had the ABILITY to do just a LITTLE BIT "BETTER" than the "BEST"...Give just a little bit MORE than the "REST". When you KNOW NO LIMITATIONS, you will EXCEED EXPECTATIONS ♥ Do not accept "ORDINARY" when definition has been given to the word "EXTRAORDINARY"...allow this "EXTRA" to "define" YOU ♥ (LCF)

Lauren Christine Frahn

FAITH OF THE MUSTARD SEED

♥ You are INCONSEQUENTIAL...when compared to your POTENTIAL ♥ While we may feel as if we are SMALL, we are capable of ENORMOUS things...through God. The Bible tells us that all we NEED is FAITH the size of a "MUSTARD SEED" ♥ Only the size of a "DOT", yet there is a TREMENDOUS lesson to be learned from this little "SPOT". Despite the INCREDIBLE task of having to grow up to fifteen FEET, there is no question that it will ACHIEVE its "FEAT"! ♥ Some may choose not to "hear it", but you can not FLOURISH without taking the time to "NOURISH" your "SPIRIT". Putting God FIRST in your life and giving Him your implicit TRUST is a MUST, for He is the "SOURCE" of GOOD and the common TRAIT among all things GREAT ♥ Whenever "tense", remember that your ABILITY is IMMENSE. If you experience "frustration", follow the SEED's "illustration"...and never "CEDE" to less than what you are CAPABLE of ♥ When you have an "INKLING" of DOUBT, follow the "symbol" of the SPROUT! BELIEVE in the ABILITY of your inner "SPORE" and you will SOAR. To ACHIEVE the GROWTH that you are able to ATTAIN, "Implant" in your brain the TRUST of this "GRAIN" ♥ (LCF)

Words Beneath Wings

FIND YOUR "FEEL-GOOD"

♥ Experiencing feelings of NEGATIVITY simply means that your WELL-BEING has WANDERED...Don't worry, it hasn't gotten too FAR...immediately set out on the SEARCH to FIND YOUR "FEEL-GOOD" ♥ If you are experiencing sadness, FIND all of the things that bring JOY into your life...and summon back your SMILE ♥ When you are stressed, allow yourself a moment to RELAX and return safely to a place of TRANQUILITY ♥ When loneliness tries to SEEK you, hide behind your CHEER ♥ Bring back ALL of your sources of HAPPINESS that temporarily "ESCAPED" your thoughts in order to send anger on its way! ♥ The REWARD for finding your "MISSING" feelings of POSITIVITY is PLEASANTNESS... Always be on the QUEST to locate your BEST ♥ (LCF)

Lauren Christine Frahn

FITNESS FOUNTAIN OF YOUTH

♥ Discover the FOUNTAIN OF YOUTH through FITNESS ♥ You are only as old as you FEEL - Feel your absolute BEST by keeping your BODY at its best. By staying in top SHAPE, you not only benefit the HEALTH of your HEART, but you stay "YOUNG at heart". You ENABLE yourself to always continue to do the ACTIVITIES that you love, which keeps your spirit ALIVE. Enlivening your SPIRIT keeps your mind INVIGORATED, giving you the ENERGY to zip through your days with a GET-UP-AND-GO energy ♥ Sustaining your POWER through training EMPOWERS you...MIND, BODY and SOUL ♥ Fitness is VITAL to keeping your VITALITY! Crack your YOUTH CODE with cardio and curls! MAINTAINING your MUSCLE maintains your MOXIE! ;) ♥ (LCF)

FLAP YOUR WINGS OF POSITIVITY

♥ The "movement" of "FLAPPING your WINGS", created by offering words that ENCOURAGE and performing actions that UPLIFT, creates a MOVEMENT that will have an "INFINITE" impact on a "COUNTLESS" number of people ♥ Make the MOST of your circumstances and you will be sure to INSPIRE others to do the same. Lead like a noble "MONARCH" so that everyone who is SUBJECT to your "POWER" of POSITIVITY will favorably EMULATE what you "DICTATE". Like the BEAUTY of the BUTTERFLY, captivate the attention of others through your CHARM and GRACE...and set an amazing SEQUENCE in place ♥ By the "nature" of this process, ELEVATING the SPIRIT of others will have you, too, "SOAR" to new HEIGHTS. Thereafter, whomever comes into CONTACT with those on which you have had an IMPACT are not "COCOONED" to this phenomenon...Whether near, far, or "ACROSS THE MAP", they will feel the effects of your FEEL-GOOD "FLAP" ♥ To create this incredible "FOLLOW-THROUGH", understand that The BUTTERFLY EFFECT begins with Y-O-U. IMAGINE THE WINGS...IMAGINE the POSSIBILITIES" ♥ (LCF)

Lauren Christine Frahn

61

FOR GOODNESS SAKES!

♥ Make a "CONSCIOUS" effort to follow your CONSCIENCE. Live with "VIRTUE" and always stay "TRUE" to Y-O-U ♥ Be "UPSTANDING" by "STANDING UP" for what you BELIEVE...and never DECEIVE. To be "UPRIGHT", you must not "LIE"...In order to hold your head HIGH ♥ SINCERITY is "essential" for PROSPERITY. To attain RESPECTABILITY, INTEGRITY is "integral", so being JUST is a "must" ♥ Realize the VALUE of your "VALUES"...Do not "interrupt" the WEALTH of your "WORTHINESS" by being CORRUPT, for you will end up spiritually "bankrupt" ♥ Stare "down" the OPPOSITION who tries to alter your UPRIGHT "position". It will be much easier to go "toe-to-toe" with this "opponent" than the one that you will have to "contend" with in the mirror if you allow yourself to participate in a "match" of IMMORALITY ♥ Maintaining your BIRTHRIGHT is reason alone to be "FORTHRIGHT", so don't be "NONSENSICAL" and do what is "ETHICAL"...For "GOODNESS" sakes! ♥ (LCF)

FORCE A NEGATIVE TO A POSITIVE

Never permit PRESSURE to "weigh you down" or allow "STRESS" to stop you in your "tracks"...Use the FORCE of the emotions that you are feeling and add FUEL to your PRODUCTIVE "fire" ♥ Make it a point to never allow STRAIN to RESTRAIN you from taking ACTION... use it to add SPRING to your step and TACKLE a TASK with all of your MIGHT! When you can turn a potentially DESTRUCTIVE temperament into one that is CONSTRUCTIVE, you will not only BOOST your mood, but also your WORK RATE! ♥ Take charge of INFLAMED feelings by using their CHARGE to work FOR you and not AGAINST you...TRANSFORM the INTENSITY from "negativity" by PROPELLING yourself into something POSITIVE! ♥

FORGET TO REGRET

♥ How "STRONG" are you? REGRET is the HEAVIEST "weight" in the world...how much have you been "carrying"? ♥ While the goal in weightlifting is to "break down" the muscles, WOE is not the "LOAD" that you want to use...the only thing you are "breaking DOWN" is your body's WELL-BEING. You must RELAX in order to remove this TAX on your body. "Put down" the BURDEN of this unnecessary STRIFE...and "LIFT" your LIFE! ♥ Understand that EVERYTHING that you have experienced this far has carried a lesson, and with that lesson, comes WISDOM. Every single event has "SCULPTED" you into WHO you are today and has brought you to WHERE you are right now...this is EXACTLY where you are intended to be ♥ The "road" of REMORSE is not the COURSE that you want to take...Do not "miss giving" all that you can to your life by having MISGIVINGS ♥ The time is NOW to release the STRAIN of your mental BALL-AND-CHAIN... REMEMBER that in order to make progress, you must "FORGET TO REGRET" ♥ (LCF)

FROM "BOTTOM-TO-TOP"

♥ When it comes to SUCCESS, more important than how far you can GO is what you do with a "LOW"! A favorable "OUT-come" depends on your ability to "OVER-come" with agility! The question is not how close you get to the "ground", but how "HIGH" is your "REBOUND"? ♥ Often, a "BOTTOM" is placed before getting to "the TOP"...Do you keep on going or just give up and STOP? When you "FALL" SHORT of the plan that you set out to ATTACK, will you stay on your knees and "SLACK" or immediately BOUNCE BACK? ♥ Even the GREATEST of "fighters" have had to deal with a "knock-out"...will you "TAP OUT"?...OR never claim "defeat" and GET BACK ON YOUR FEET?! Never "choose" to "LOSE"! For the ultimate championship's "prize", you must DECIDE to RISE! ♥ "ROCK-BOTTOM" is only a TEMPORARY "situation" that you can use for your goal's REJUVENATION...will you use this to "build" an even stronger FOUNDATION or "raze" the project out of fear and HESITATION? Will you COWER under the "weight" of TOIL or use your "power" to RECOIL? Even if you find yourself in the deepest VALLEY, do not "dilly-dally", but start a "comeback" RALLY! ♥ When you enter your "BOTTOMMOST" STATE, in order

Lauren Christine Frahn

to accomplish all things GREAT, you must quickly RECUPERATE! Take a situation that may be considered "DIRE"...transform it into "BACKFIRE"...and LAUNCH yourself to ACHIEVE the plans that you DESIRE! ♥ If your "DREAM-boat" becomes "capsized", your success can still be "realized"! No matter how deep you may "sink", your feet will eventually touch the FLOOR... so PUSH OFF and SOAR to HIGHER levels than ever before! ♥ When a "DEAD END" is where you "arrive", the intensity of your DRIVE will determine whether your dream can SURVIVE...Keep your HOPES "alive" by always striving to THRIVE and forcing your SPIRITS to "REVIVE"! It is up to Y-O-U to always "PULL THROUGH" and START ANEW! ♥ (LCF)

Words Beneath Wings

FROM WORRY TO WORTHY

♥ DREAMS start with an idea that you BELIEVE in, but you must also believe in YOURSELF...More important than an INTENTION's "inception" is your SELF-PERCEPTION ♥ There is "no room" for a LACK of CONFIDENCE. If you feel UNCERTAINTY "crowding" the "gala" of your GOALS, show them the "exit door"... SKEPTICISM and SUSPICION are always "uninvited guests"! As soon as you "see them out", REFOCUS on your ultimate "VISION" and get back to the "celebration" in honor of your ASPIRATION ♥ "Upgrade" the seat of your PSYCHE to "FIRST-CLASS" and "travel" past your FEAR by getting "clear" on your CAPABILITIES, using this MORALE to "transport" you to the farthest "locale" ♥ EXPECT the very BEST of yourself...Never limit your attainable "ALTITUDE" with an ATTITUDE of INCERTITUDE ♥ Fortify any "deficiency" in your SELF-SUFFICIENCY by replacing an opinion of WORRY with the FACT that you are WORTHY...because you ARE ♥ (LCF)

Lauren Christine Frahn

"Your life happens NOW...The REST OF YOUR LIFE is based on what you do with your "NOW" MOMENTS"

FUTURE = PRODUCT OF OUR PRESENT

♥ In today's culture, there is so much EMPHASIS placed on IDEALS that it becomes very easy to live just for the ATTAINMENT of those "idealized" FUTURE goals. However, you must not forget about the SIGNIFICANCE and IMPORTANCE of your CURRENT MOMENTS, for it is these very moments in the HERE and NOW that are CREATING your FUTURE ♥ Failing to TAKE THE TIME to make the MOST of your PRESENT creates an injustice NOW that will EXTEND into the years ahead. However, NURTURING each and every moment and making it as SPECIAL as possible, will create a future that "follows suit" ♥ It is only when we are GRATEFUL for our EXISTENT situations in life that life can give us MORE things to be grateful for ♥ Remember, the rest of your life is a "PRODUCT" of your PRESENT..."MULTIPLY" the possibilities EXPONENTIALLY by making each and EVERY moment "COUNT" ♥ (LCF)

Lauren Christine Frahn

GET BACK ON THE BIKE!

♥ If you have ever ridden a BIKE before, it doesn't matter HOW LONG it has been, you can GET BACK ON without forgetting how to PEDAL! The same is true when it comes to WORKING OUT! Your MUSCLES have "MEMORY" and will be able to get BACK to where they were in a FASTER amount of time than when you originally started TRAINING...regardless of HOW MUCH time has passed, your muscles haven't "forgotten" you ;) ♥ DECIDING to "get back on the bike" is the hardest part...after the initial pedal, you're BACK TO SPEED in no time! ♥ Find the MOTIVATION that IS lying within you...Do not be intimidated...you've done this ALL BEFORE! If necessary, grab a partner as your "TRAINING WHEELS" to provide an added sense of SECURITY. Soon, you will be back in the RHYTHM, training wheels or not! ;) ♥ Do not delay "STEERING yourself" to the path of OPTIMAL HEALTH..."GET BACK ON THAT BIKE"...and pedal like you've never pedaled before! ♥ "BACKPEDALING" with EXCUSES gets you NOWHERE...Release the hand brake of HESITATION and get "back to the speed" of SUCCESS and ACCOMPLISHMENT! ♥ (LCF)

GET-UP-AND-GO!

♥ SELF-DOUBT is the biggest impediment to ACHIEVING one's SUCCESS. It can force you to "INCH forward" when, in fact, you have the ABILITY to "move" MILES! Taking it one "step" further, this DOUBT can prevent you from even putting one "foot" in front of the other! Remember, however, that the only thing that you should be stopping "in its tracks" is this LIMITING MINDSET ♥ Well, this is your WAKE-UP call! The "hibernation" of your GOALS is over! The life that you have to this point only DREAMED about can NOW be your REALITY. It is time to "ARISE" to the AMAZING life that you are INTENDED to live! "GET-UP-AND-GO" get started on ALL of the things that you were created in order to ACCOMPLISH! ♥ BUILD UP your BELIEF in yourself by taking "BABY STEPS" toward your goals. Your "CAN-DO" attitude will GROW exponentially with each one, as will the SIGNIFICANT "struts" that you develop the CONFIDENCE to take ♥ Y-O-U are capable of so much MORE than you may realize...REALIZE this in order to REALIZE YOUR POTENTIAL ♥ (LCF)

Lauren Christine Frahn

GIVE IN TO YOUR GREATNESS

♥ APPRECIATE IN VALUE by APPRECIATING YOUR VALUE!! ♥ Do not "obey" ORDINARY, nor "pay any mind" to MUNDANE, for Y-O-U are CAPABLE of SIGNIFICANCE! ♥ It is so important to understand the incredible WORTH that lies WITHIN each and EVERY one of you. Do not "surrender yourself" to SUBPAR with SELF-DEPRECATING "self-talk" when, in reality, you DESERVE THE BEST! ♥ If you DOUBT this to be TRUE, chances are that you are NOT where you could and SHOULD be in life...Well, guess what?! We've just identified the problem! If you find that you "shy away" from SUCCESS out of FEAR of CHANGE, understand that who you are comes from WITHIN, not in WHAT you do, so stop "giving in" to MEDIOCRITY out of this fear! You are CAPABLE of so much MORE than COMMONPLACE...as soon as you DECIDE for yourself that you ARE! ♥ There is no reason to ever cause yourself to "fall short" or to "fear FANTASTIC", for you are PHENOMENAL...GIVE IN TO YOUR GREATNESS! ♥ (LCF)

GUNG-HO!

♥ While a THOUGHT does create a THING, being INACTIVE accomplishes...NOT A THING! To change ANYTHING, you must DO SOMETHING! ♥ If you are not happy with any given CIRCUMSTANCE, it will not improve by leaving it to CHANCE. For a PREDICAMENT to IMPROVE, you must MAKE A MOVE! ♥ There is no PROSPERITY in INACTIVITY! For PRODUCTION worthy of SATISFACTION, you must first TAKE ACTION! For results that are ATTRACTIVE, you must be PROACTIVE! Do not just mosey along, but COME ON STRONG...Performance that is IMPRESSIVE requires you to be AGRESSIVE! ♥ ACHIEVEMENT that is AMAZING does not happen from "LAZING"! To realize a life that is ABUNDANT, you cannot be RELUCTANT...In order to "tackle" any FEAT, you must move your FEET! ♥ Remember to not allow a nega-tive EMOTION to prevent you from putting your-self in MOTION. Understand that WORRIMENT is an IMPEDIMENT to ACCOMPLISHMENT! An attitude of WOE leaves you no room to GROW...To make the most of LIFE, forget about your STRIFE and remember to KNOW that you must be GUNG-HO! ♥ In order to make life the greatest CELEBRATION, you must first come

Lauren Christine Frahn

out of "hibernation"! Do not "sleep" on your opportunity to live with ANIMATION and EXHILARATION! It is "crazy" to be LAZY, so "quit" being "berserk" and get to WORK! ☺ ♥ (LCF)

"Do not accept "ORDINARY" when definition has been given to the word "EXTRAORDINARY"...allow this "EXTRA" to "define" YOU"

Lauren Christine Frahn

HABITUATE TO GREAT!

♥ To IMPROVE a talent from good to "GREAT", you must learn to HABITUATE...Perform the ACTION until you have total SATISFACTION ♥ Have the WILL to put your "SKILL" on a "DRILL" for a "FINESSE" that is sure to IMPRESS! For EXCELLENCE "BEYOND COMPARE", tend to your CRAFT with "repetitive" CARE. SHARPEN your TECHNIQUE to the "FINEST" of "points" for a PRECISION that never "disappoints"! Your "RHYTHM" and STACCATO will ultimately evoke cheers of "BRAVO!" ♥ PERSISTENTLY TRAIN to CONSISTENTLY ATTAIN your IDEAL "development". No matter how many "TRIES", the REPETITION of an "EXERCISE" will eventually help you to achieve the results that you IDEALIZE! It is important that you never "loosen your grip", because eventually you WILL get the "HANG OF IT"...Maintain an attitude of APTITUDE! ♥ Remember, you cannot SLACK if you want to PERFECT your KNACK. To "produce" RESULTS that are "A-OK", go through a "DRY RUN" of your FORTE each and EVERY DAY! "TUNE INTO" your "GIFTS" on constant REPEAT in order to have them be continuously REPLETE ♥ For a LINE that is "FAULTLESS", do not slip through a "crack" by decid-ing to take a step BACK! To prevent your ABILITY'S "reversal", be sure to consistently RUN THROUGH a

DRESS REHEARSAL! PRACTICE "over time" will make your SAVVY "SUBLIME"! ♥ Until the day that you find "proof" that life will provide you with a DO-OVER, be sure to "GO OVER" your FLAIR until it is "FOOLPROOF"! Remove any "hesitance" to settle for less than EXCELLENCE...and POLISH your "ART" to PERFECTION, without exception! ♥ In order to "go places", "WALK THROUGH" your WORK until it is "ACES"! Remember, REDUNDANCY leads to EXCELLENCY...Create the PHOENIX of your GENIUS ♥ (LCF)

Lauren Christine Frahn

HALF-FULL GLASS OF WONDER-FULL

♥ PAY ATTENTION to what you "DESIRE" while allowing thoughts of what you don't want to "EXPIRE"... Dismiss negativity and PERMIT POSITIVITY ♥ There are "two" ways to look at ANY given situation... always choose "one" of ELATION, without hesitation! ♥ CHOOSE to "look" on the BRIGHT SIDE in order to LOSE "sight" of a DIM VIEW...Wear only "ROSE-COLORED GLASSES" so that the "DARK SIDE" always passes ♥ "Disallow" SADNESS in order to "give way" to GLADNESS...Remove thoughts of FEAR to allow the PRESENCE of CHEER ♥ Whether your VIEW is "impressive" or "depressive" is strictly up to YOU. There is no reason to blame OUTSIDE circumstances when your "OUT-LOOK" is an "INSIDE" job ♥ "OPT" only FOR "OPT-IMISM" for the "OPT-IMAL" quality of life ♥ Do not "let yourself DOWN" with a DOWNCAST disposition...reposition to an "UP-beat" tone in order RAISE your "LOW" SPIRITS and "ELEVATE" your mood ♥ "Segregate" from SORROW for a better TOMORROW...It is okay to "discriminate" against "hate"...Never "hesitate" to "designate" only attitudes that are "GREAT" in order to POSITIVELY PREDESTINE your "fate" ♥ MAKE UP YOUR MIND to see life the way God intended that you should...and TRANSITION your entire life for the GOOD! ♥ Always DECIDE to see the "glass" HALF-FULL for a life that OVERFLOWS with "WONDER-FULL" ♥ (LCF)

HAVE MERCY!

♥ ABSOLUTION is the RESOLUTION to the "strain" of DISDAIN ♥ For "EASY" dealings, remove "HARD" FEELINGS. Remember, YOU are the only one that has to bear the DRUDGE of "holding" a GRUDGE. In releasing another person from your RESENTMENT, you are actually freeing YOURSELF to move on with CONTENTMENT. RANCOR will only put on "anchor" on YOUR progress...MAKE PEACE with any "pain" and remove its BALL AND CHAIN! ♥ Understand that FORGIVING does not say that a wrongdoing is "okay", but that you refuse to CARRY around the "weight" for one more day. LIFE IS TOO SHORT to "tote" around the burden of another's "TORT" ♥ Giving RESPITE does not indicate that you are DESPERATE, for it is only the alternative that will leave you feeling "DESOLATE". Offering REPRIEVE for a PEEVE in no way means that you are being "naive"...You are actually more MATURE for not allowing the burden of BITTERNESS to ENDURE ♥ Granting PARDON does not mean that you no longer CARE, but that you have decided to replace the "pollution" of a TRANSGRESSION with a "breath of FRESH AIR". Take COMPASSION by the "reins" in order to prevent BAD BLOOD from entering your VEINS

♥ Time goes too FAST to spend your precious moments hindered by LOADS from the past...Do not FORGET, but leave no room for REGRET ♥ Ironically, there is no greater FREEDOM than that which comes from GRACE's "embrace". Give eternal "WINGS" to your SOUL through the liberating TRANSFORMATION of VINDICATION ♥ For the best of days, HAVE MERCY "all-ways"...and allow your SPIRIT to SOAR "forever-more" ♥ (LCF)

Lauren Christine Frahn

HE IS IN THE ROOM

♥ How would you act if Jesus were IN the room WITH you? ♥ Would your ACTIONS be different? Would you SPEAK in a different manner? Would you treat others BETTER? ♥ With His footsteps inches from yours, you would be sure to put your "BEST foot forward"? With His VOICE within "earshot", yours would only "reverberate" with KINDNESS, HARMONY and LOVE. With His HANDS an "arm's length" away, you would be much more prone to "reach out" yours to HELP those in need ♥ In vividly imagining His PRESENCE right next to yours, your SPIRIT SOARS, taking you to a HEIGHT where you vocalize VIRTUE, act with BLESSED behavior and carry only a DIVINE disposition. As often as possible, act and speak "AS IF" He is standing "IN THE ROOM"...because HE IS ♥ (LCF)

HIT THE "GAS PEDAL"!

♥ When taking on a new VENTURE or in PURSUING something that you never have done before, it is common to experience feelings of APPREHENSION. Typically, what causes this ANXIETY is the "UNKNOWN", along with the concern of FAILURE ♥ While SUSPICION can often be an alert of "danger", you must understand that in cases like this, it is NOT a WARNING SIGNAL! You must not allow this TREPIDATION to STOP you "in your tracks"! ♥ When you start to feel that FEAR is giving you a "RED LIGHT", do not "step on the breaks" of your DREAMS! Take a second to picture the END RESULT of the GOAL in your mind and allow this EXCITEMENT and DETERMINATION to WARM up those "COLD FEET"! ♥ FUEL your actions with your FAITH... Allow your PASSION for your project to "rev your engine"...and HIT the "gas pedal" of your PURSUITS! ♥ (LCF)

HIT YOUR "RESET" BUTTON

♥ In LIFE, as in BOWLING, sometimes it is good for your "pins" to get KNOCKED DOWN. If you never experienced moments that HURLED you off of your feet, you wouldn't be able to APPRECIATE all of the WONDERFUL times ♥ Serving a BENEFIT as they do in the bowling alley, these kinds of "STRIKES" can BOOST your "PERSONAL SCORE" and have a POSITIVE compounding effect for the following "FRAMES" of your LIFE ♥ The important thing to remember is that when situations like this occur, you mustn't allow yourself to stay "IN THE GUTTER". Use these occasions as OPPORTUNITIES to press the "RESET" BUTTON on your "LANE" of life and determine how you will use the NEXT "BALL" to HIT A SPARE...BOOM!! ♥ (LCF)

HOOK, LINE & SINKER!

♥ The creation of your REALITY begins with your THOUGHTS ~ "BAIT" your "HOOK" properly! ♥ COGNITIONS will bring the identical EXHIBITIONS into your life. You will "ATTRACT" back a certain "fish" based on the "LURE" that you USE, so be very SELECTIVE with the one that you CHOOSE! Before "CASTING" your "LINE", make sure the "CHUM" is "IN line" with the EXACT fish that you would like to see COME! ♥ EXPECT only the BEST for yourself and have your ACTIONS follow suit with those thoughts. If you want the "BIGGEST" fish in the OCEAN, do not select a "ROD" that cannot handle the "MOTION"! ♥ BELIEVE yourself to be capable of attracting the grandest fish of the "SEAS"...IMAGINE bass and trout, without thoughts of minnows or anchovies! Do not allow your thoughts to "BOB" up-and-down as to what you are DESERVING of. Believe yourself to be worthy of the most "prize-winning" "GAME"...and that is exactly what you will "REEL IN" ♥ If you "CATCH" yourself thinking negative thoughts, simply "RELEASE" them and refocus on "PULLING IN" POSITIVITY. "TURN THE TIDE" of life in your favor by looking for the "UPSIDE" in all circumstances ♥ Become a "MAGNET" for all things AMAZING! You do not have to travel in a "SCHOOL" to be aware that your MIND is your greatest "TOOL"...use it to "TACKLE" life, "HOOK, LINE, & SINKER!!" (LCF)

Lauren Christine Frahn

85

HOW MUCH ARE YOU WORTH?

♥ "STRIVE" to be "ALIVE"...While it is important to work hard to attain SUCCESS, there is nothing in this world that has more VALUE than your "VITALITY"! ♥ It truly does not matter how "WELL-OFF" you are if you don't have your "WELL-BEING". A LAP OF LUXURY "means" NOTHING if you don't have your "MEANS"! You may LOVE your POSSESSIONS with all of your "HEART", but you are only truly REPLETE when you make sure that it maintains its "rhythmic BEAT" ♥ The greatest ASSET you possess is that which "HOUSES" your PERSONAL PROPERTY...There is no "measure" for the superior TREASURE of its "UNDERLYING" FORTUNE. A SOUND BODY and MIND are the greatest RICHES you will ever find! ♥ Your "HEALTH" is your greatest "WEALTH"...How much are you WORTH?!" (LCF)

I CAN'T BELIEVE THIS!

♥ Right beyond your "shade" is a LUMINOUS "glade"... stop focusing on your "PLIGHT" and walk towards the "LIGHT" ♥ In an occasion of sorrow, remember that the SUN will come out "tomorrow"...Replace "sadness" with "gladness" by TRUSTING that moments causing "TEARS" of JOY are on their way! ♥ If feeling "concealed" beneath feelings of "BLAH", have FAITH that your moments of "A-HA!" will soon be "revealed". Do not assume a "costume" of GLOOM, nor don DESPAIR's "disguise"...just KNOW that God is soon to transform these limited "LOWS" to lengthy "HIGHS" ♥ If in a "slump", be SURE that you will soon make it "over the HUMP"...When a burden seems too "HEAVY" to "bear", rest assured that you will soon feel as "LIGHT" as "AIR"! ♥ If you can't get a "clear picture" of life and all seems to be "STATIC", have NO DOUBT that you will soon have reasons to be "ECSTATIC"!! Get your MINDSET "on the mend", for HAPPINESS is right "around the bend"...Do not feel "slighted", but get EXCITED! ♥ Never "UNDER-estimate" your intended level of HAPPINESS, for you were destined to be "OVER-joyed". THINK yourself "tickled pink"...and "lose" the "BLUES"! ♥ Remember,

Lauren Christine Frahn

HOPE is never "lost"..."find" yours using the sense of "CLARITY" that DREAMS do become "REALITY"! ♥ BELIEVE that you will soon have "I CAN'T BELIEVE THIS!!" moments because..."TOO GOOD TO BE TRUE!" is just the START for you!! ♥ (LCF)

ILLUMINATE YOURSELF
THROUGH OTHERS

♥ Sometimes it feels hard to cast away DARKNESS in your mind, but you are not CONFINED to its SHADOW... you must PUSH yourself to SHINE THROUGH ♥ Even if you currently feel that you are blind to the SHIMMER of BRIGHTER feelings, you must determine to immediately make moves to find this SHEEN. CONCENTRATE your efforts on seeking CHEERFUL interactions with others. By forcing yourself to shine LIGHT on those around you, it will automatically REFLECT back to ILLUMINATE YOU ♥ WILL YOURSELF to SEE...in finding RADIANCE outside you, you will FEEL radiance WITHIN ♥ "Break free" from GLOOM by bringing forth the GLEAM of GLADNESS in others and in turn, create a BEACON of LIGHT for YOU to find your way back to ♥ (LCF)

Lauren Christine Frahn

IMPACT

♥ Every individual ACTION can bring another individual "satisfACTION". Would you think about your "ACTions" differently if you KNEW that every single thing that YOU DO has an "impACT"? ♥ The way that you "AFFECT" even one person has the ability to "INFECT" countless others..."spread" PROSPERITY! ♥ Always AIM TO "IMPRESS"..."ASSESS" your behavior to verify that it is helping others to reach for "SUCCESS"! ♥ "APPRAISE" your actions on a daily basis to "ensure" that you are giving "PRAISE"...and helping others to "RAISE" their bar ♥ Taking even the smallest of "steps" with GOOD DEEDS has the ability to TRANSFORM into "WELL-BEING" "stampedes" ♥ When you make others "RADIANT", their "light" will SHINE on all who cross their "path"...leaving a "contagious" GLOW in the "aftermath" ♥ Counteract any "contention" and INTERACT with good INTENTION ♥ "SIZE UP" your efforts to verify that your "EXTRA-LARGE" garments of KINDNESS always "fit" "JUST" "RIGHT" ♥ Avoid "SOUR GRAPES", so as not to leave a "bad taste" in another's mouth ♥ You do not need "affluence" to make a significant "INFLUENCE", but simply the ability to MAKE A "DIFFERENCE" ♥ Do not "discount" your ability to "SWAY", for even your most "ROUTINE" of gestures "COUNT" from day to day, so make every "SOLITARY" move EXEMPLARY... the resulting number of "INDIVIDUALS" that you will INSPIRE is "extra-ORDINARY" ♥ (LCF)

Lauren Christine Frahn

IT'S WHAT YOU DON'T SAY

♥ Be AWARE of what you are saying...WITHOUT SPEAKING a single WORD ♥ COMMUNICATION is the FOUNDATION of all good relationships, so it is vital to understand that the majority of the MESSAGES that you send are SILENT ♥ When INTERACTING with others, your facial expressions, gestures and even your posture convey SIGNALS that often speak LOUDER than words. Approach every ENCOUNTER with a POSITIVE mind frame so that you, in turn, become APROACHABLE. ACT in an "UPRIGHT" manner in order to have your head held similarly. BE ENGAGED in your conversation so that your eyes ENGAGE the other. Be FIRM about demonstrating your CARE to others and have your HANDSHAKE follow suit. BE GENUINE, making sure that your WORDS and ACTIONS match up, for it is very hard to fake your body LANGUAGE ♥ Always make the MOST of your WORDLESS SIGNALS...WHAT YOU DON'T SAY, SAYS SO MUCH ♥ (LCF)

"JUST ENOUGH" IS NOT ENOUGH

♥ Unless you are doing ALL that you CAN, you are not doing AS MUCH as you SHOULD ♥ Make the very MOST of your ABILITIES by making USE of them to do AMAZING things. There are those in the world without these ENDOWMENTS who would do anything in the world to have the OPPORTUNITY to be ABLE to do what you ARE ABLE to ♥ To "CHEAT" your EFFORTS is to cheat YOURSELF from ALL that is POSSIBLE for Y-O-U! Do not take your CAPABILITIES "for granted", for being COMPETENT is a granted BLESSING ♥ Fully UTILIZE your TALENTS in order to fully REALIZE your POTENTIAL...NO EXCUSES! ♥ MAXIMIZE your CAPACITY to do GREAT things..."JUST ENOUGH" IS NOT ENOUGH ♥

Lauren Christine Frahn

93

KEEP ACCELERATING

♥ Once you have determined the ideal DESTINATION that you would like the "ROUTE" of life to lead you to, step on the GAS PEDAL! ♥ With your AMBITION in mind, you want to hit the "GROUND" running, but it is not necessary to "FLOOR" it! While the universe does respond well to SPEED, it is not necessary to get in a "RACECAR"...Just be sure that you are in DRIVE! ♥ Obey the "TRAFFIC" laws, keep your eyes on the "ROAD", and take it one "MILE" at a time. Getting pulled over for a "speeding" VIOLATION will only DELAY your "arrival". Remember, "shortcuts" don't pay off in the end...Do not burn yourself out by trying to "BURN RUBBER"! ♥ Tune out any "BACKSEAT" drivers telling you that you are going the wrong way...Y-O-U are the only one with the accurate GPS on this trip. There are sure to be some "BUMPS" along the way, so "STRAP" on your "SEATBELT"...allow your PERSISTENCE to serve as your "SHOCKS and STRUTS" and absorb the "impact"... The "KEY" is to keep ACCELERATING! ♥ (LCF)

KEEP CLIMBING

♥ On the "CLIMB" to your SUCCESS, you are likely to encounter someone who wants to "loosen" your "footholds"...KEEP CLIMBING ♥ There are those who will voice their OPINION that they do not understand or believe in your goals, but you must STAY FOCUSED and "hold on" tightly to the "MOUNTAIN" of your DREAMS. CONTINUE YOUR ASCENT...If every entrepreneur allowed a critic's opinion to STOP them "in their tracks", we would not have any of the tremendous ADVANCES that we have in ALL fields of life ♥ Some will not participate in the ENJOYMENT of seeing you SUCCEED...Do not permit them to "drag you down" your "CLIFF". Maintain a FIRM GRIP on your "ropes" of DETERMINATION and make sure that you OUT CLIMB any "juggernaut" ♥ No matter who tries to "pull you off" of your mountain, you are "HARNESSED" by your FAITH. Keep your eyes FOCUSED on the APEX, for you are mere "steps" away from the amazing VIEW from the TOP...and ALL of the MANY who can't wait to APPLAUD you at the SUMMIT! ♥ ♥ (LCF)

Lauren Christine Frahn

KNOCK ON OPPORTUNITY'S DOOR

♥ There is NO ONE else that can carry out what God created YOU specifically to do... FIND A WAY to MAKE IT HAPPEN ♥ God believes in YOUR ABILITY to ACCOMPLISH this GOAL, for you were the "CHOSEN ONE" for this task. If you have an idea, understand that you cannot use the excuse that you "don't know" where to start...you have been GOD-GIVEN this very IDEA as your STARTING POINT! ♥ Your intended PURPOSE is yours, and yours alone, to PURSUE and to ACHIEVE. You'll never get your "foot in the door" playing "ring-and-run" on your door of OPPORTUNITY... God placed an enormous WELCOME MAT there for you...STAND ON IT! ♥ With this in mind, never take "no" for an answer, for God has ALREADY established the "YES" for you. Don't wait for "opportunity to knock", but KNOCK ON OPPORTUNITY'S DOOR...if no one answers, KNOCK IT DOWN! (Just be sure to put it back on the hinges!) ;) ♥ (LCF)

KNOWLEDGE IS POWER

♥ Maintaining an ACTIVE body is priority, but don't forget to TRAIN your BRAIN! ♥ Along with every CALORIE you BURN, keep your fire going with a YEARN to LEARN. CHALLENGE your MIND daily by introducing it to a new EXERCISE...It is the greatest MACHINE that you will ever UTILIZE ♥ Feel your BEST by always seeking new information to DIGEST...a heavyweight MENTAL WORKOUT feels GREAT! There is not a more positive STIMULATION than that of an ever-growing EDUCATION. When you keep your mind EXPANDING, you will INCREASE the feelings of JOY that go hand-in-hand with UNDERSTANDING ♥ KNOWLEDGE is POWER...MAXIMIZE your STRENGTH by picking up as much INFORMATION as you can handle ♥ (LCF)

Lauren Christine Frahn

"LICKETY-SPLIT" LUXURY

♥ We are in a society TODAY where things need to "happen YESTERDAY"...technology is undoubtedly SPEEDING UP the expectations for the amount of time required to achieve "REWARD" ♥ However, adopting an "OLD-FASHIONED" mentality when it comes to FULFILLMENT can be beneficial, for GRATIFICATION is not always INSTANT. That which is WORTHWHILE is worth WORKING towards. Just because you cannot derive ENJOYMENT from something IMMEDIATELY does not mean that it is not WORTHY of your EFFORTS ♥ SATISFACTION is not always SPLIT-SECOND...in fact, the GOALS that you work HARDER to achieve, for LONGER periods of time, are typically the ones that deliver the most DELIGHT. Do not base your ASPIRATIONS simply on the ones that might produce "LICKETY-SPLIT" LUXURY, for those are often the ones that LACK sustainable JOY ♥ RELAX your desire for DIRE results... it is the UNHURRIED outcomes that produce the most PLEASURE ♥ (LCF)

LIFE OF F.A.M.E.

♥ It is a "WELL-KNOWN" fact that making a positive IMPACT simply requires you to be a person of TACT... You need not be a "CELEBRITY" to treat others with "INTEGRITY" ♥ You do not have to be a "SUPERHERO" in order to be another's everyday "hero", nor a famous "PERSONALITY" to extend common "COURTESY". You need not be a "BIG NAME" ...to remember someone's "name". You do not have to be a "BIG CHEESE"...to say "thank you" and "please". A monument in your honor need not be somewhere "on DISPLAY"...to wish some-one a "GOOD DAY". You do not have to sell out shows on a worldwide TOUR...to hold open a DOOR. Your name need not be on a MARQUEE...to bring another smiles and GLEE ♥ A "BIG DEAL" of EMINENCE is not necessary to make a "big deal" of DIFFERENCE. You do not have to be "LARGER THAN LIFE" to be a "giant" influence ♥ A "SPOTLIGHT" is not required to bring LIGHT to another's life. You do not have to be "ELEVATED" in order to "raise" another's spirits. A "BIG GUN" is not essential in order to "take aim" at helping someone ♥ Being "RECOGNIZED" is not a prerequi-site in order to "recognize" the GOOD in others. You do not have to be "TALKED ABOUT" to "talk about"

Lauren Christine Frahn

others with PRAISE, nor must you be "APPLAUDED" to give another a "round of applause" ♥ You do not have to be "NOTED" to make a "noteworthy" impression. You do not have to be a "STAR" to encourage others to "reach for" one ♥ Often, it is the efforts AWAY from the "LIMELIGHT" that provide the most "LUSTER". Go the "EXTRA" mile in all things "ORDINARY"...and affect others in an "EXTRAORDINARY" way ♥ To be "FAMOUS" is not necessary in order to be "FABULOUS"...Live a life of "F.A.M.E." in EVERY WAY!: "F.abulously A.ffect M.any E.veryday" in EVERY WAY"! ♥ Remember, a "V.I.P." status is not required to make other's feel that they are "V. ery I.mportant P.eople" ♥ (LCF)

LIFT A "HEAVIER" WORKLOAD

♥ You are CAPABLE of so much MORE than you may give yourself credit for ♥ We are creatures of ADAPTATION, both PHYSICALLY and MENTALLY. When you FORCE a MUSCLE to carry additional WEIGHT, it reaches FATIGUE at first, but with proper TIME and CARE, it will eventually GROW. In the very same way, when you CHALLENGE your MIND with a "heavier" WORKLOAD to ACHIEVE higher GOALS, you will ADAPT to this additional "weight"! With time, this will GROW your SUCCESS and ultimately, "LIFT YOUR LIFE"! ♥ "MAX OUT" your EXPECTATIONS of what IS POSSIBLE for you...You CAN "HANDLE THE WEIGHT"! ♥ (LCF)

Lauren Christine Frahn

"Every day, strive to be just a little bit better than the you that you were yesterday...and GROW YOURSELF TO GREATNESS."

LIMITLESS POTENTIALITY

♥ Conviction in your COMPETENCE is of utmost IMPORTANCE. What does your "means" mean to you? The "ALTITUDE" of your APTITUDE is in your ATTITUDE ♥ Keep your thoughts "on track"...Never "derail" yourself from a tenacious "TRAIN" of thought by believing that there is something that you cannot ATTAIN. "Generate" a positive "COMMOTION" with your steadfast "LOCOMOTION"...and always move "FULL STEAM AHEAD" ♥ Work up a "perspiration" when going for your ASPIRATION, but when it comes to your ADEQUACY, maintain a "NO SWEAT" mentality ♥ The extent to what you can ACCOMPLISH depends on the belief that your EFFICIENCY is HONORABLE...Do not set your "MAXIMUM CAPACITY" at a "lower" number than what is TOLERABLE ♥ The POTENTIAL that is "bottled" within you should never be "contained"..."unscrew" the "CAP" on your POSSIBILITIES ♥ IMAGINE BIG and DREAM BIGGER, for the ABILITY within Y-O-U is BIGGEST...LIMITLESS "POTENTIALITY" is your CURRENT "REALITY" ♥ (LCF)

Lauren Christine Frahn

LOVE "AS IS"

♥ LOVE is UNCONDITIONAL...not "under the condition" that one CONFORMS to your PROTOTYPE ♥ In order to TRULY love someone, you must love him or her for who THEY ARE and not for who you would LIKE them TO BE. Understand that you cannot CHANGE anyone but YOURSELF, nor should you attempt to... you are the ARCHITECT of your own UNIQUE blueprint, not that of another's ♥ Attempting to ALTER another is not ADORATION...true AFFECTION is based on his or her AUTHENTICITY, not on a FACADE that only favors YOUR FANCY ♥ Truly loving another does not involve TRANSFORMING them into someone that satisfies YOUR wants and desires. To LOVE an individual is to RESPECT them, and that includes his or her INDIVIDUALITY ♥ Love APPRECIATES and ACCEPTS "AS IS", not "IF WHEN" ♥ (LCF)

LOVED AND "LOST", BUT HOPE IS NOT

♥ Just because you have LOVED and "LOST" does not mean that YOU are lost...Perhaps the greatest QUEST of your life is JUST BEGINNING ♥ When a relationship comes "TO TERM", not on YOUR terms, you will certainly go through a period of sadness, but do not let that turn to despair, for HOPE is NEVER "ASTRAY" ♥ You must first FIND YOURSELF...and then set out to DISCOVER why it is that this particular relationship went "MISSING"...there is always a REASON, and it is ALWAYS a GOOD one ♥ Hey, as AMAZING as Y-O-U are, the only one who really lost is the one who "went WANDERING" ;) ♥ When love "STRAYS", I assure you that there is an even DEEPER and better LOVE just waiting to be FOUND. You must never give up HOPE, for to "call off the SEARCH" prematurely would be to give up one of the greatest REWARDS you will ever realize...a LIFETIME SUPPLY of TRUE LOVE ♥ (LCF)

Lauren Christine Frahn

MADE IN THE U.S.A.!

♥ As an AMERICAN CITIZEN, there are so many reasons to be PROUD, so declare your "national anthem" ALOUD...and make it your "PREROGATIVE" to be POSITIVE! ♥ Salute your "STAR-SPANGLED BANNER" in an HONORABLE MANNER, for there is SO much you CAN DO simply by being a part of the "RED, WHITE & BLUE"! Around every corner, opportunity "lurks", so always be striving to "SPARK" your inner "FIREWORKS"! ♥ Utilize your INDEPENDENCE by taking huge "strides"... You are the only one who DECIDES whether your LIFE is the most amazing of "rides"! It is both "idiotic" not to be PATRIOTIC and "crazy" to be LAZY when you reside in the great LAND OF OPPORTUNITY!! J In our DEMOCRACY, you do not have to be "regal" to SOAR like an "EAGLE"! Remember, UNCLE SAM WANTS Y-O-U to EXCEL in ALL that you DO!! ♥ Why settle for "a little" when you can achieve A LOT in this magnificent "MELTING POT"?! Do not hold on to trivial "gripes", but make the most of being a part of the "STARS & STRIPES"! Let go of any "strife", because ANYTHING that you DREAM of can be your LIFE! ♥ PLEDGE your ALLEGIANCE to "LADY LIBERTY" and never take for granted the PRIVELEGE of your SOVEREIGNTY. CHOOSE

Words Beneath Wings

106

the PURSUIT OF HAPPINESS and "refuse" your right to be a "CRANKY YANKEE"...REJOICE with GLEE that you live in the "LAND OF THE FREE"! ♥ The "odds" are in your FAVOR by being a proud "FLAG-WAVER", so never "gamble" with the PREAMBLE! Y-O-U were "MADE IN THE U.S.A.!", so "Capitalize" on your "LAISSEZ-FAIRE" by GOING FOR every DREAM that you can possibly DARE! By "REALIZING" ALL that your BIRTHRIGHT does bring, your heart is sure to "sing"..."LET FREEDOM RING"! ♥ (LCF)

Lauren Christine Frahn

MAKE A S.H.I.F.T.

♥ In order to "scale" higher mountains in your life, you have to be willing to REFORM the way you "climb". If you desire to "RAISE YOUR BAR", you must "ALTER" what you have done in the past in order to take your life to this HIGHER LEVEL ♥ In order to make the "TRANSITION" to your new "AMBITION", you must also have the "ambition" to "transition" YOURSELF. You can not RENOVATE your "style" if you continue to wear the "clothes" that always have...you must REFASHION your "wardrobe". To "build" bigger DREAMS, you must be willing to RECONSTRUCT your current "blueprints" ♥ The only way to REMAIN "commonplace" is if you DETAIN yourself by keeping your current "pace". Once you RETAIN new methods to "advance", SUSTAIN your progress by making a "tweak" each and every week ♥ Remember, a "stick shift" is necessary to CHANGE "gears", but you must also stick with this "S.H.I.F.T"..."Success. Happens. If. Followed. Through." ♥ (LCF)

MAKE TIME FOR YOUR DREAMS

♥ SCHEDULE in order to MAKE TIME...ARRANGE your AGENDA so as to be able to follow ALL of your PASSIONS ♥ PRIORITIZE which activities will help you to ACHIEVE your goals...and eliminate those that will not ~ Do not be a "servant" to time, but make USE of your time to BEST SERVE YOU ♥ Putting a PLAN together for your day is putting a plan together for the REALIZATION of your GOALS and ultimately, for your LIFE. WRITE DOWN what you want to ACHIEVE, and then list the DAILY steps that will be REQUIRED in order to MAKE them happen as SOON as possible. GET EXCITED about each completed task, for each CHECK MARK means that you are "ON your mark" towards attaining your DREAMS...Get your life "in CHECK"...do not "miss your MARK" ♥ SET AN ALARM for yourself to get a JUMP-START on your PLAN of ACTION for the day...Don't "SNOOZE" on your OPPORTUNITY to make the MOST of each and every day by hitting its "button" ♥ Each of us has the ABILITY to CREATE and PLAN the life of our DREAMS. Time doesn't WAIT around, however, so neither should Y-O-U ♥ Time is what you MAKE of it...MAKE the best use of yours ♥ (LCF)

Lauren Christine Frahn

MAKE YOUR MARK DARK!

♥ You have only ONE LIFE to develop your "BRAND" ...make your "LOGO" worthy of RECOGNITION ♥ Be "resolute" in this single PURSUIT and "clever" in every ENDEAVOR because you do not get another "TRY" once your days have "GONE BY" ♥ Take a "second" before making a "first" IMPRESSION to make sure that this IMPACT is one of "TACT"...and remain "INtact". Be sure that your "REPUTATION" always leaves a positive "INDENTATION" ♥ Create a "STAMP" that will "stick" only to "FIRST-CLASS" mail ♥ Trying to "navigate" through life "under the radar" is a "mistake"...Make your "location" UNMISTAKABLE by setting your "DIRECTION" with a POSITIVE PURPOSE... ON purpose...and create CONSEQUENCES...OF "consequence" ♥ It takes only ONE FINGER to count the number of CHANCES you get to LIVE YOUR LIFE... leave a FINGERPRINT of fabulousness ♥ "There is no DO-OVER in the "walk" of life, so OVER-DO your efforts at leaving a PROMINENT "FOOTPRINT" ♥ God appointed YOU as your own personal "proctor" in the "TEST" of life... fill in its "circle" completely...and make your "MARK" DARK! ♥ (LCF)

"MASTER" ARCHITECT
OF YOUR DREAMS

♥ When God "ENGINEERS" a DREAM inside of your heart, the DESIRE to PRODUCE it will "DEMOLISH" any "obstruction" that tries to "OCCUPY" this "FOUNDATION" ♥ Do not ignore this "BLUEPRINT"! Even if you try to walk off of the "JOB", its "CONSTRUCTION CREW" will always bring you right back. There is not a better "GENERAL CONTRACTOR" to execute these PLANS than the one appointed by its "DIVINE DESIGNER", and that is Y-O-U ♥ Embrace this OPPORTUNITY that has been ORIGINATED within you. It is not only a chance to "INSTITUTE" an even better life for yourself, but likely in the lives of many others well. Often, in "BUILDING" your ENTERPRISE, several UNIONS are formed that also realize the "BENEFITS" ♥ Put down any "MONKEY WRENCH" that is not prop- erly assisting you and "RAZE" any doubts that have been "raised". You must "REALIZE" that it is a "PLAN" that ultimately KNOWS NO FAILURE...The "MASTER ARCHITECT" has already laid its "FRAMEWORK" ♥ (LCF)

Lauren Christine Frahn

M.O.P. UP A SPILL

♥ Why throw a STUMBLING BLOCK on the "track" when the "straightaway" to your FEAT's "FINISH LINE" is "hurdle-free"? ♥ Do not allow your thoughts to HARBOR "stormy" seas when the view to the "port" of the destination of your DREAMS is pleasantly PLACID ♥ When striving for FIVE-STAR "cuisine", do not "COOK UP" a "recipe" for DISASTER ♥ FABRICATING a "snag" will cause your feet to "drag". Allowing your brain to "draw" depictions of "RESTRICTIONS" only creates "sketches" of SKEPTICISM and AFFLICTION. ♥ APPREHENSION leads to INACTION, a "Catch-22" which ultimately produces "0" SATISFACTION. When on the road to your GOALS, you must always "persist", so do not INVENT "inter-FEAR-ences" that do not "exist" ♥ The very greatest of ACHIEVERS must also have been BELIEVERS, for their successes did not come without INTERRUPTIONS...they simply overcame the numerous OBSTRUCTIONS ♥ In order to fulfill your ASPIRATIONS, you must "clean" your mind of CLUTTER. Remember, "IF" you are faced with a "spill", just "M.O.P." it up!: "Meet. Overcome. Persevere!" ♥ (LCF)

MORAL JACKPOT

♥ Do not "GAMBLE" with your CHARACTER by REPEATING unwanted actions or behavior, but WIN at the" game of life" by using a STRATEGY that will IMPROVE your "game" DAILY ♥ If you behaved in a way that you didn't like, or did something that you wish you hadn't, "all bets are NOT off"! Every day is a NEW OPPORTUNITY to put the "ODDS" back IN YOUR FAVOR ♥ Just because you "DEALT" yourself a "BAD HAND" one time does not mean that you have to continue on that "LOSING STREAK". While it is okay to hit the occasional "CRAPS", just be sure that the NEXT time you are "handed" the SAME "DICE", you ROLL them in a DIFFERENT way...it is in REPEATING the behavior that will COST you all of your MORAL "CHIPS" ♥ Each night, take the time to review in your mind how you would have done things DIFFERENTLY, picture the WINNING RESULT...and HIT YOUR "MORAL JACKPOT" tomorrow! ♥ (LCF)

Lauren Christine Frahn

MUCH ADO ABOUT...YOU!

♥ Things that BOTHER us in OTHERS are often the very ones that "IRRITATE" us about OURSELVES...Before you open your mouth with a negative "inflection", consider whether this is actually a "self-REFLECTION" ♥ If you feel yourself about to "complain", determine the source of the "STRAIN" and use this "AGGRAVATION" as a cue for "self-EXAMINATION". A "PAIN IN THE NECK" usually means it's time to get YOURSELF "in check"! ♥ If a part of "society" has caused you an "ANXIETY", do not send yourself into a "FLURRY" of "WORRY", but realize that this is "much ADO about...YOU!" ♥ Take the time spent "scrutinizing" others and instead use it in "analyzing" yourself...As an "ANNOYANCE" draws nearer, take a step back and look in the "mirror". Eliminate these traits that throw your ideal character "off track", for the only IMAGE you can change is the one staring "back" ♥ "Pointing your finger" at a PEST is a signal to put yourself "to the TEST"...Before you CHOOSE to "ACCUSE", perhaps this is a lesson that YOU could "use"! ♥ (LCF)

MUTE YOUR SHOWBOAT'S HORN

♥ If you are teeming with "TENACITY", do not have the "AUDACITY" to be overly "AUDIBLE"...it is much more respectable to be "RESERVED" than in making a point to be "OBSERVED"! When you GLOAT and "blow the horn" of your own SHOWBOAT, the "sound" is not always pleasing to the ear. While you may think that "turning UP" your "VOLUME" will get you better NOTICED, you are likely turning people "OFF"! ♥ Leave others "speechless" by way of SILENT SPIRIT and not "at a loss for words" due to a POMPOUS presentation ♥ SELF-RELIANCE speaks VOLUMES when its expression is "MUTED"! ♥

Lauren Christine Frahn

NEVER SEESAW WITH A RHINO

♥ VENTURE with those who "ENHANCE" your "ADVANCEMENT" and do not serve as an "IMPEDIMENT" or a "DETRIMENT" to your "BETTERMENT" ♥ Guarantee "EVOLVEMENT" by giving your "INVOLVEMENT" only to those who "COMPLEMENT" what you "DESIRE"... and "HIRE" these individuals that will help you "GAIN" what you hope to "ATTAIN" in your "CAMPAIGN" ♥ In pursuing your "DREAM", make sure that you "TEAM" up with those who "TEEM" with your same level of "STEAM". "PAIR UP" with those who don't play "games" that could CAUSE your CAUSE to "FLARE UP" in "flames" ♥ Give your GOAL treatment that is "ROYAL" by "building your castle" with those who are "LOYAL"...A prosperous "PARTNERSHIP" requires a "PARTNER" that will not "jump SHIP"! ♥ In anything you "UNDERTAKE", there must be "GIVE-AND-TAKE". Do not put your "operation" AT STAKE by "joining forces" with those who do not PARTAKE in the "duties" necessary to complete your overall "mission" ♥ A successful "CORPORATION" requires "COOPERATION"...Permit PARTICIPATION only to those who give your PROGRESS a "boost" without trying to OVERRULE your "roost" ♥ Enter a "TRANSACTION" with someone equally as "VESTED" on the outcome, so as not to become "DIVESTED" on what you "INVESTED". Be wise when you "STRATEGIZE" and "employ" the right "guys" that will enable you to "REALIZE" your "ENTERPRISE" ♥ Do not choose a "CLOWN" or a PARTNER that will "drag you down"... Wouldn't it be "PREPOSTEROUS" to try to "seesaw" with a "RHINOCEROS"?! Instead, OPT for someone who is "GREAT" and knows how to "pull their WEIGHT"! ♥ Only "put your chips" on those who are not afraid to go "ALL IN" to bring your dream to reality..."Roll the dice" on those who have "WHAT IT TAKES"...and "UP YOUR STAKES!" (LCF)

NOTE YOUR PROGRESS...
AND PROGRESS

♥ If you feel that you are at a STANDSTILL and that your efforts are no longer making PROGRESS, you are at a critical point in time, for you have two options...ONE CHOICE...that will literally CHANGE your life. Are you going to QUIT or are you going to CONTINUE your JOURNEY? ♥ Do not allow your FRUSTRATION to overpower your WILL. Think back to where you were when you originally set out to ACCOMPLISH your task...chances are that you HAVE MADE some pretty decent HEADWAY, right? Now imagine where you will be when this same span of time ELAPSES again and add PEP back in your STEP! You have no reason to be DISHEARTENED...rather, get your HEART back IN the process...and PROGRESS ♥ On the "straightaway" to your DREAMS, do not get overwhelmed if your STRIDES suddenly seem to be STATIONARY. Rather, look back to take note of HOW FAR you have traveled and then CONTINUE to GAIN GROUND...SUCCESS is so much CLOSER than you may think ♥ (LCF)

NO VACCINE FOR VIGOR

♥ Be RESPONSIBLE for the PRESENCE that you CREATE ♥ Always aim to have a POSITIVE IMPACT on the people that SURROUND you ~ Take a second BEFORE you ENTER anywhere that you will encounter others and DECIDE to bring only FAVORABLE ENERGY ♥ It feels so much BETTER to leave a room knowing that you've left your COMPANY in a BETTER STATE than when you arrived ♥ POSITIVITY and SMILES are "CONTAGIOUS" if you carry enough of the "FEEL-GOOD germ"..."SPREAD" it wherever you go, leaving behind "SYMPTOMS" of UPLIFTED spirits, SMILES and JOY! ♥ Start a "WELL-BEING EPIDEMIC" by deciding to "INFECT" others with your ENERGY...We don't need a "VACCINE" for VIGOR! ♥ (LCF)

Lauren Christine Frahn

NO WORRIES

♥ WORRY doesn't serve as a "remedy" for anything... ALLEVIATE your APPREHENSION with ACTION ♥ ANXIETY is not something that happens TO you, for it is self-induced...YOU bring it upon yourself with your THOUGHTS. In the same manner, you can LET IT GO by switching your FOCUS. Often, your ANGUISH results from the ANTICIPATION of a future event that may... OR MAY NOT...occur. Do not spend valuable time "IN FEAR" over a situation, but get "IN GEAR". REASSURE yourself with the mindset that no matter what may come your way, you WILL handle it in the BEST way that you can when (and IF) it presents itself. Take COMFORT in knowing that you only have CONTROL over your PRESENT...stressing over "non-events" not only doesn't serve you, but it solves nothing. RESOLVE that you will SOLVE any situation that arises in order to effectively DISSOLVE your unnecessary fear ♥ Replace WORRIMENT with EMPOWERMENT...and LET GO of the WOE ♥ NO WORRIES ;) ♥ (LCF)

"You only have your LIFETIME, so have the TIME of your LIFE! Money is VALUABLE, but MOMENTS are INVALUABLE"

Lauren Christine Frahn

"NOW" MOMENTS

♥ It is okay to use the "IF-and-WHENs" in your life as your GOALS, but do not forget the "HERE-and-NOWs", for they are the only GUARANTEE ♥ It is important to not only MAKE the very MOST of the PRESENT DAY, but to also BE PRESENT. Do not "stare" too far down the "road of LIFE" and allow yourself to be OVERWHELMED by imagining there to be "BUMPS" ahead. SMOOTH the "pavement" with the realization that these "PROJECTIONS" may not even happen! ♥ Avoid "falling into" the "POTHOLES" of worried thought by staying FOCUSED on the PRESENT. Decide that you will HANDLE every situation to the BEST of your ABILITIES...and keep TODAY open for ALL of its POSSIBILITIES ♥ The "TRIPLE AAA" way to create the BEST possible DAY is by making the MOST of everything that comes your way...AS IT COMES. Remember, your life happens NOW...The REST OF YOUR LIFE is based on what you do with your "NOW" MOMENTS ♥ (LCF)

NOWADAYS THE BESTADAYS

♥ Don't wish for the days of the PAST, for when you live in your YESTERDAYS, you lose your TODAYS, which CREATE your TOMORROWS ♥ If your days of YORE were better than your present, YOUR job is to determine why...it is up to YOU to do your best to make every day BETTER than the LAST...and then make them last. It is up to you to make your "NOWADAYS" the "BEST-A-DAYS" and not live in your "THEN-A-DAYS" ♥ Living in a "remember when" state means that you are failing to see all of the AMAZING things that are EVER-IMPROVING all around you. The world is constantly ADVANCING...EMBRACE the change! Starting now, leave behind your 'OLD LANG SYNE' mindset and convert to one of 'CARPE DIEM' ♥ Do not let another day go by living in your "days gone by"...The "GOOD OLD TIMES" should be the ones that you are CREATING TODAY ♥ (LCF)

Lauren Christine Frahn

NUTS ABOUT Y-O-U!

♥ APPRECIATION for your CURRENT SITUATION is the only way to make the GRADUATION to a "higher" YOU ♥ Create a "STANDUP" position by "FALLING FOR" your present DISPOSITION. Why go "crazy" trying to be someone that you are NOT, when you should "BE WILD" about the TRAITS that you HAVE GOT?! Never find disappointment with your "appoint-ment" in life, but "BE MAD ABOUT" your "tem-per-ament"! ♥ The only way to make FORWARD progress is to be "STUCK ON" your present "loca-tion" with genuine "ADORATION". A sustained inner "DRIVE" requires your ADMIRATION, so give yourself a "STANDING" OVATION...and never take a "backseat" to BETTERMENT ♥ Always strive to get your "grass" a little "greener", but do not fail to take notice of the VIBRANCE of your current "DEMEANOR". "FERTILIZE" your CHARACTER with GRATITUDE, while pulling out "weeds" of WOE...and watch how quickly you GROW! ♥ In a "nutshell", you can only go "far" when you cherish the person that you ARE...so be "NUTS ABOUT" Y-O-U!! (LCF)

"OH HAPPY DAY!"

♥ CHOOSE the OPPORTUNITY every day to "DIAL" yourself in to becoming the BEST that you can be...now, hit the "SEEK" button and look for an UPBEAT "sound-track" ♥ "FIND" the way to see the "GIFT" in every-thing that life "presents" you with...and be PRESENT ♥ Take the time to recognize the MIRACLES that surround you, allowing the MAGIC to fill your heart with GRATITUDE...and reflect this in your ATTITUDE ♥ Life will "cater" to your THOUGHTS and "dish up" events throughout the "course" of the day that con-tain SIMILAR "seasonings" to your REASONINGS, so make sure that these thoughts "serve" you...and look to SERVE others ♥ There is no "measure" to the amount of PLEASURE that results from an endeavor to provide a GOOD DEED for someone "in need". Count on the fact that your helping hand "writes a check" which your HEART always "approves"...and make MOVES ♥ Take "steps" toward ACHIEVING your DREAMS and GOALS. No matter how small you may deem them to be, ADVANCEMENT is always "immense"...now MAKE GREAT STRIDES ♥ The moment is HERE and your "station" is now CLEAR...Turn up the volume and press "Play"...."OH HAPPY DAY"! ♥ (LCF)

Lauren Christine Frahn

125

ON PURPOSE

♥ Without a PURPOSE, it doesn't matter which PATH you choose to take in life because the truth is, all will eventually lead you "SOMEWHERE"...the question is whether this "somewhere" is "OVER THE RAINBOW" or just "OUT THERE" ♥ Without a clear VISION of what you want to ACHIEVE, the course of your life resembles a LABYRINTH...the right way could be ANY way because the path to your DESTINATION is UNKNOWN! Set up a "TARGET" goal on which your soul can "AIM" and maintain only a "Bull's-eye" focus on this DREAM ♥ Point yourself in the right DIRECTION by setting an INTENTION to accomplish your heart's AMBITION...and give MEANING to your life's MISSION ♥ You cannot just "wish upon a star", but you must SET YOUR BAR...and "ASPIRE" to always raise it "HIGHER". Give PURPOSE to your life... "ON" purpose ♥ (LCF)

ONE SCHEME TO MOVE FULL STEAM

♥ Major ACCOMPLISHMENTS all have one thing in common...they all start with a single THOUGHT. It takes only ONE IDEA to COMPLETELY change your life ♥ If a current lack of PROGRESS has you feeling frustrated or dreary, remember that all it takes is just ONE THEORY to "whisk" you away to SUCCESS...BRAIN"STORM" to create these "winds" of CHANGE ♥ Your dreams do not require "magic potions"...all that is needed is just ONE of your special NOTIONS. Never EXTINGUISH the "flames" of your creative CONCEPTS, for the very next one could be THE one that will DISTINGUISH you from the rest ♥ A single SCHEME can take you full STEAM ahead. Always keep your "WHEELS TURNING"...you may very well be only a couple of "rotations" away from TURNING YOUR LIFE AROUND ♥ (LCF)

Lauren Christine Frahn

ONE AT A TIME, PLEASE!

♥ You will FIND the greatest sense of SATISFACTION when you SEEK your GOALS, but it is crucial that you do not attempt to "tackle" them ALTOGETHER. Pursue your various PASSIONS and HOBBIES in order to fully DEVELOP your WELL-ROUNDED CHARACTER, but it is not necessary to "MAKE THEM HAPPEN" all AT ONCE! ♥ Keeping yourself CHALLENGED is necessary in order to GROW, but there is a "fine line" between keeping yourself BUSY and taking on TOO MUCH..."BIDE your time" and PRIORITIZE in order to avoid "crossing over" that "DIVIDE" ♥ While VARIETY is the "spice" of life, adding too much to your "plate" will eventually remove the "taste" and JOY from the experience ♥ When it comes to your DREAMS, avoid "clowning" around by throwing too many "balls" in the air at ONE TIME...Successfully "JUGGLE" your GOALS one (or two!) at a time! ♥ (LCF)

ONE ROCK AT A TIME

♥ Before making your "TO-DO" list, "think twice" before trying "to-do" TOO MUCH "at once" ♥ While there is nothing that is "TOO MUCH" when it comes to your DREAMS, trying to "stuff" too much into the "garments" of your GOALS will cause them to rip at the "seams". There is a big difference between "filling your cup" to OVERFLOWING and "loading your plate" to OVERWHELMING ♥ To create a "surPLUS" of results, do not "ADD" too many "factors" to your "equation" of SUCCESS...Doing so will "SUBTRACT" from the final "RESULT" that you have "calculated" in your mind ♥ A capacity OVERLOAD will eventually cause its "container" to "EXPLODE". "BUILD UP" your GOALS, but lay them "brick-by-brick" so as to avoid a "BREAK DOWN" ♥ You can "MOVE MOUNTAINS", but only one "rock" at a time, so to be PRODUCTIVE, you must remember this INDUCTIVE "rhyme": What you can ACHIEVE is "EXPONENTIAL", but a "near-sighted" focus is "ESSENTIAL" in order to MAGNIFY your "POTENTIAL"! ♥ (LCF)

Lauren Christine Frahn

OPPOSITES DO NOT ALWAYS ATTRACT

♥ OPPOSITES do not always ATTRACT ♥ There are times in life when you may be CRITICIZED for who you are...Keep your feet in their firm "position" and STAND UP against this CONTRAPOSITION. If "attacked" for what you BELIEVE in, keep up your "defenses" against this COUNTERATTACK ♥ Everyone has different "tastes"...stay TRUE to your "palate" and never "stretch" your "OUTLOOK" in order to "reach" the "VIEWS" of those on the "OTHER SIDE". Do not "flip a quarter" to determine a DIFFERENT answer than the one that you already know in your heart to be yours simply to "appease" the "OTHER SIDE OF THE COIN" ♥ Never CONFORM to someone else's "standards", but be sure that you always hold yourself to the HIGHEST of yours...and keep your head held in that very same manner. Remember, it is your UNIQUE thoughts, opinions and behaviors that make you the "crop's cream"... Do not forgo this "classification" by "converting" to the "OTHER EXTREME" ♥ Never permit an ANTITHESIS to determine your "THESIS" in life. You are a "ONE-and-ONLY", therefore "only" you can write your one "EXPOSITION"...Write it with "CONVICTION"...and rise above the "OPPOSITION" ♥ (LCF)

Words Beneath *Wings*

"The "ALTITUDE" of your APTITUDE is in your ATTITUDE"

Lauren Christine Frahn

OPTIMISTIC EXPECTATIONS

♥ When starting the "process" of achieving your goals, do not allow your mind to PROCESS an "absence" of PROGRESS...Focus only on the "presence" of PROBABILITY ♥ Of course, it is "easy" to get overwhelmed if you are LOOKING FORWARD with the ASSUMPTION that this chosen course will be "hard"... Provide "relief" with an ENCOURAGING BELIEF ♥ Be sure that you have only a "sunny" OUTLOOK and do not FORECAST "storms" ahead ♥ Improve your ABILITY by thinking only of "positive" POSSIBILITY. Make certain that the CALCULATION of your PREDICTED outcome is "exponential" and "factors out" any "negative" results ♥ Replace a VIEW that is "ominous" with the "light" that is PROMISE...Have only OPTIMISTIC "EXPECTATION" for your motive's "manifestation" ♥ Positive EXPECTANCY is the "key" to unlocking the "doors" to your dreams. Replace the "defiance" of doubt with the "compliance" of "self-RELIANCE"... TRUST is a "must" ♥ (LCF)

PEOPLES' RIGHT-OF-WAY

♥ Your WORK-AT-"HAND" should never take prece-dence over taking the time to hold another's...Never choose a GOAL over a LIVING SOUL ♥ Spending time with another for ENJOYMENT should supersede a constant EMPLOYMENT. There is a major difference between a "FOCUS" on your OCCUPATION and allow-ing a PRE-OCCUPATION with it to blur your "vision" toward another HUMAN BEING ♥ Pursuing your DREAMS is undoubtedly DIVINE, but your ATTENTION TO OTHERS should always be "first in LINE". While it is a remarkable quality to be highly DRIVEN and "DILI-GENT", prioritizing another GAL or GENT is far more "intelli-GENT"! ♥ Pay attention to what another ASKS instead of "tuning them out" so as to finish other TASKS. What someone has to SAY should always "outweigh" your work-"load" for the DAY! An ACTIVITY with the ones that you ADORE has far more QUALITY than any DUTY or CHORE ♥ Never provide a "busy signal" to another's "CALL" in pursuit of your "CALLING". "Pay NO MIND" to your DAILY GRIND if one that you hold DEAR needs to "borrow your EAR". Being a good "FRIEND to" another is far more important than any ERRAND that you have to "TEND to" ♥ It is UNMISTAKABLE that

Lauren Christine Frahn

relationships are BREAKABLE, so "handle them with CARE" if you would like them to always BE THERE. If need be, your ASPIRATION can wait...it does not come with an EXPIRATION date! Remember, a dream in your heart is not DESTROYABLE, so "dividing" your attention to others will "exponentially" make the journey more ENJOYABLE ♥ PEOPLE should always have the "RIGHT-OF-WAY" over any "matter" that comes your way...There is no OPPORTUNITY that is worth the "cost" of being LONELY ♥ (LCF)

PERPETUAL ENHANCEMENT

♥ Never stop "GROWING" ♥ While physical GROWTH is "limited", your PERSONAL DEVELOPMENT is UNINHIBITED ♥ Be of STRONG BODY. Stay ACTIVE in order to "HIKE UP" your PHYSICAL capacity and always ELEVATE your ENDURANCE to "new heights" ♥ It is "common KNOWLEDGE" that you must FEED your BODY in order to GROW, but getting the proper "NOURISHMENT" of KNOWLEDGE is just as "essential" so that your BRAIN's "BUILDUP" doesn't "slow". Look for ways to stay MENTALLY CHALLENGED, so as not to "defy" LOGIC ♥ Keep an OPEN MIND to all of life's POSSIBILITIES, so as not to CLOSE yourself OFF from all of your CAPABILITIES. There is never an end "in sight" as to the NOVELTIES available to you, so BROADEN your "horizons" by always LEARNING something NEW ♥ "FILL" your HEART with TENDER, LOVING CARE to ensure that it's PRODUCTION of AFFECTION will always be there. Maintain a WARM and FEEL-GOOD "environment" with conditions that will serve to FOSTER its SENTIMENT ♥ STRENGTHEN your FAITH in order to SUSTAIN your BEAUTIFUL SOUL, so that the GRACE of your SPIRITUAL BEING will never "take a toll". Maintain a CONSCIOUS "involvement" with your BELIEFS to

Lauren Christine Frahn

135

guarantee EVOLVEMENT of your CONSCIENCE ♥ For a "journey" of life that is DIVINE, always be on a "mission" to REFINE. When you stay "WELL-ROUNDED", you will be "ASTOUNDED" at what becomes possible...PROGRESS is LIMITLESS ♥ "Never-ending" ADVANCEMENT leads to "perpetual" ENHANCEMENT ♥ Never stop IMPROVING ♥ (LCF)

PERSONAL RIVALRY

♥ Comparing yourself to others does not "serve" you... The only person you need to "obSERVE" is Y-O- and U. In order to get an ACCURATE self-assessment, you must "SEGREGATE" from the "aggregate" ♥ The best PROGRESSION requires the "recognition" that YOU are your only "OPPONENT"...BE ACCOUNTABLE for your "private" ACTIONS without allowing "outside" distractions. To ensure your ADVANCEMENT's "survival", you must remember that YOU are your only "rival"... Put yourself to the "test" to ACHIEVE a daily "personal BEST" ♥ When you "strategize" for individual ADVANCEMENT, never "compromise" this necessary ENHANCEMENT... To "SIZE UP" your "COMPETITION" and see where you "stand", the only effective way is to take your OWN "measurements" FIRSTHAND ♥ In order to be able to look at yourself with admiration and DEFERENCE, you do not require any other point of "REFERENCE"..."HOLD A CANDLE" only to your "face" in order to effectively "illuminate" your "brightest" GRACE ♥ In striving to be "more", simply aim to be BETTER than the YOU from the day "before". Make sure that your efforts "STACK UP AGAINST" the ones from the day "prior"...and then make that "heap" a little HIGHER ♥ To make the "vision" of the OPTIMAL

Lauren Christine Frahn

you "clearer", only "MEASURE" yourself against the person staring back at YOU in the "mirror"...the true WIN of this day in and day out "trial" is if that very reflection is "wearing" a SMILE ♥ GROW YOURSELF TO GREATNESS ♥ (LCF)

"CHOOSE to "look" on the BRIGHT SIDE in order to LOSE "sight" of a DIM VIEW...Wear only "ROSE-COLORED GLASSES" so that the "DARK SIDE" always passes" (LCF)

Lauren Christine Frahn

PERSPECTIVE IS YOUR ELECTIVE

♥ "Picture" an ERRAND as "effortless" and a CHORE no longer a "bore"...It's all about your "FRAME of reference"! ♥ Transform your ACTIVITIES into "FESTIVITIES"! Make your "GRUNTWORK" feel like "STUNTWORK"! Switch aggravation into "CELEBRATION" by converting a "kick in the shins" to a "SHINDIG"! ♥ Find a way to "unwind" in your "DAILY GRIND" and turn an OCCUPATION into "RECREATION"! Your PRODUCTION should not be a "WORKOUT", but a "NO SWEAT" PROFESSION. Choose the "right" ANGLE so that you are not "left" in the dark! Make the "light" of a "HEAVY" DUTY so "bright" that you can "BASK" in the TASK! ♥ Life it not meant to be a "RAT RACE", but a "journey" to EMBRACE...not a "pursuit" of LABOR, but a "venture" to SAVOR. "Convert" your "CONTEXT" so as to ENJOY the "contest"! ♥ Choose an "UPBEAT" tempo to "march" through the "parade" of life and then enjoy the "VIEWPOINT" from this "GRANDSTAND"! ♥ "OPT for an "OBJECTIVITY" of POSITIVITY...PERSPECTIVE" is your ELECTIVE♥ (LCF)

PICK UP YOUR PACE

♥ If you are AWARE that you are LIMITING your "pace", BEWARE that you are "ON PACE" to LIMIT your POTENTIAL ♥ You KNOW when you are not reaching the SPEED that you have the ABILITY to because the thought of ACHIEVING what you TRULY yearn for makes your HEART beat so much FASTER. If you know you are CAPABLE of MORE, why in the world are you SETTLING for less?? ♥ MOVE with the "GAIT" that you have been DESTINED to in order to open the "GATEWAY" to your dreams. Never "TROT" when your MIND is at a full "GALLOP", and when your SPIRIT wants you to "RUN", don't "STROLL"...CHOOSE to CHASE your ultimate GOAL! ♥ Let nothing SLOW you down from CAPTURING what has CAPTURED your SOUL ♥ (LCF)

Lauren Christine Frahn

PIGSKIN PROGRESS

♥ In order to make PROGRESS down the "FIELD" of your DREAMS, you must always have a STRATEGY in order to ADVANCE, and not just leave it to "CHANCE" ♥ You are the "head coach" in charge of creating your "PLAYBOOK" ~ When determining the next "PLAY CALLS" for your "QUARTERBACK", do not cut any "slack"...choose the ones that will MOVE you toward the "END ZONE" as EFFICIENTLY as possible. Keep in mind that it is typically the GRADUAL, yet productive "CARRIES" that will "march" you from the "FIELD OF PLAY" over the "GOAL LINE" ♥ PAY ATTENTION to the "PLAY CLOCK", keeping a steady PACE, and avoid looking for the "quick" and "easy" SCORE...It is extremely rare that a "HAIL MARY" pass will give you the "TOUCHDOWN" that you are after and can often lead to a game "disaster". Make sure that your "TEAM" is "WELL-EQUIPPED" and keep your head "IN THE GAME". Trying to "RUSH" the ball without paying attention to TECHNIQUE often leads to "FUMBLES" and "TURNOVERS" ♥ When "TOSSING THE PIGSKIN", always go for the WIN. Take every day one "YARD" at a time, accomplishing "GOAL" after "GOAL"...and before long, you will have arrived at your "SUPER BOWL" (LCF)

PLANT "SEEDS" OF PROSPERITY

♥ If you plant flowers, you get flowers...if you plant weeds, you get, well, weeds! Be careful what types of "SEEDS" you PLANT in YOURSELF, for you will surely REAP what you SOW ♥ Every day, you "scatter seeds" within yourself by way of your SELF-TALK...make certain to plant seeds of ENCOURAGEMENT in order to "yield" CROPS of CONFIDENCE ♥ The longer that weeds are left to grow, the harder it is to REMOVE them, for they SPREAD and become persistent about growing back...the same is true of SELF-CRITICISM. Do not allow negativity to "spread" within you ♥ PERSIST in your efforts to give only POSITIVE self-affirmations and instead, you will GROW your "garden of GOODNESS" and REAP its RICHES ♥ Plant PROSPERITY, HARVEST HAPPINESS... and gather GREATNESS ♥ (LCF)

Lauren Christine Frahn

PLEASANT IN THE PRESENT

♥ No matter where you are on EARTH, it is a moment for MIRTH...It matters not which coast or 'zone', nor what it reads on your watch, clock, or 'phone'... The TIME to be HAPPY is NOW! ♥ Why be "waitful" for a feeling that makes you GRATEFUL? Take your GRATIFICATION off of its DELAY and find reasons to be JOYFUL "RIGHT AWAY"! ♥ Remove any dismal "haze" of your "yesterdays" with the SUNRAYS of your NOWADAYS...Make sure that your smile SHINES to create only "BLUE SKIES" and "CLOUD NINES"! ♥ Why settle with being MAD when you have "86,400" reasons to be GLAD?! Do not spend any more of your "seconds" putting off FUN and CHEER until the DAY "AFTER", but make THIS very day filled with moments of "LIGHTNESS" and "LAUGHTER"! It is an absolute FOLLY that life is not meant to be JOLLY! ♥ If you feel that a "piece" of life is bringing you "TROUBLE", turn it around into PEACE OF MIND..."ON THE DOUBLE"! Replace anything TEARFUL from "LONG AGO" with all things CHEERFUL..."PRONTO"! ♥ Your PLEASURE should be without "measure", so stop "calculating" when the appropriate DATE will be for you to allow yourself to ELATE...Stop questioning your JOY'S "WHERE" and "HOW", for the "WHEN" is right HERE AND NOW!! ♥ There is no better day to be JOYFUL and GAY, so be BLISSFUL TODAY...STRAIGHTAWAY! Never be "HESITANT" to make yourself "PLEASANT", for there is no better time than the "PRESENT"! ♥ (LCF)

POINT YOUR FINGER
AT Y-O-U

♥ Maintain POWER over your life by taking full RESPONSIBILITY for what happens in it ♥ The ability to be the effective "BOSS" of your life is instantly "terminated" the second that you look to "FIND FAULT" with events or situations OUTSIDE of yourself...the "MANAGEMENT" of your life is an INSIDE "JOB" ♥ "BE IN THE SADDLE" of your LIFE and "CRACK THE WHIP" until you are at a full "gallop"...the only thing that you will lose by trying to "PASS THE BUCK" is CONTROL over your circumstances ♥ "PULL THE STRINGS" of your vocal "chords" by speaking AUTHORITATIVELY and assuming ACCOUNTABILITY for deciding to make the BEST of ALL that LIFE has to offer. It is "WISE" to never CRITICIZE. The CHOICE to "JUMP DOWN ONE'S THROAT" only takes away YOUR "VOICE"...You cannot UPGRADE your life by choosing to UPBRAID another! ♥ You will never scale the "mountains" that you aspire to by "CLIMBING ALL OVER" others as to why YOU have not yet reached these SUMMITS in your life. The only way to "SIT ON TOP" of these "ELEVATIONS" is to TAKE CHARGE of the "OBLIGATIONS" necessary to ESCALATE to their level

♥ Anything is SURMOUNTABLE as long as you are ACCOUNTABLE, so keep your "HEAD IN LIFE'S GAME" by never passing BLAME ♥ Remember, you lose the "GRIP" on your life when you "POINT YOUR FINGER" ♥ (LCF)

Lauren Christine Frahn

POW!

♥ The FORCE of God's GRACE is more POWERFUL than anything that you will ever face ♥ There is nothing that you canNOT do with the MIGHT of God BACKING you. Any circumstance that brings "ROUGHNESS" can be circumvented by your Almighty "TOUGHNESS" ♥ When you are entered into a "bout", keep in mind that you are wearing your appointed and Anointed "gloves" of CLOUT...There is not a "contender" in the world that can beat you with God "in your corner" ♥ If you come across "choppy waters", remember that the "waves" ahead are no match for the Wonderful "Wind" that carries your "sails"...even when tumultuous "tides" try to bring RANCOR, the ANCHOR of the Lord always "prevails" ♥ Even if a LOWER "extremity" tries to get the "UPPER HAND", it loses all "grip" against your SUPREME "STRONG ARM"... Your DIVINE "grasp" can "DISARM" any HARM ♥ It is a "LOSING" BATTLE for anything that attempts to cause you to "rattle", for Eternal MOMENTUM can never be OVERCOME...Your FAITH is your perpetual POWERHOUSE! ♥ At every CHALLENGE's "beginning", starting right NOW, "_P_LAN _O_N _W_INNING"..."POW"! ♥ (LCF)

PRACTICAL MAGIC

♥ When a MINOR "situation" causes a "slight" IRRITATION, take a second to determine whether this is really worth your AGGRAVATION...Don't make a "simple spark" into an "inextinguishable blaze" by adding the fuel of EXASPERATION. Before making a "NON-EVENT" real, ask yourself, "What's the big deal?" ♥ Keep a RATIONAL "frame" of mind by looking at the "BIG PICTURE"...When you change your FOCUS, what you initially view as VEXATION can go "out of sight" with slight RELAXATION. Before you let a MIFF send you "to the moon", bring yourself "DOWN-TO-EARTH"! "Cross off" getting unnecessarily CROSS from your daily "to-do" list with a REALITY CHECK! Prevent a HEADACHE by staying LEVEL-HEADED during times of "NOISE" ♥ There is "NO USE" in giving a "job" to a needless NUISANCE....Just as quickly as you answered its "call" of DISTRESS, you can just as easily "hang up" on the HANG-UP! ♥ You don't need a trick "up your sleeve" to escape a PET PEEVE...just some PRACTICAL "MAGIC" ♥ (LCF)

Lauren Christine Frahn

149

PRECIOUS MOMENTS

♥ While it is said that 'TIME is MONEY', time's VALUE is much GREATER...You can always find a way to make more money, but there is yet to be a way to create more time...Have the WHEREWITHAL to make it COUNT ♥ Your WEALTH becomes worthless if you SPEND your days consumed by your CAPITAL, for you will eventually be spiritually BANKRUPT. The greatest TREASURE of life is life itself...it does not matter how much TENDER you GET, but how much TENDER, LOVING CARE you GIVE ♥ Focus more on your TIMELINE than on a MONEYLINE. If you think that money brings you POWER, test your strength at trying to pick up another HOUR ♥ Do not pay the PRICE of having wasted time...be sure to focus on more than FINANCE in order to give the real RICHES of life a CHANCE. You only have your LIFETIME, so have the TIME of your LIFE ♥ Money is VALUABLE, but MOMENTS are INVALUABLE ♥ (LCF)

PROCRASTINATE PROCRASTINATION

♥ The only thing you should PROCRASTINATE when it comes to your "ASPIRATION" is "PROCRASTINATION" ♥ On the TIMELINE for achieving your GOALS, make sure that it starts with TODAY'S date! Why WAIT to bring about your optimal FATE?! ♥ Remove what you ASPIRE from its "COOLING-OFF PERIOD" by "firing yourself up" to go after this "burning" DESIRE ♥ Make a successful "CONNECTION" to your PREDILECTION by avoiding any "HANGUP" ♥ "Stock" an "innovative" life for YOURSELF by taking "DISCONTINUED products" off of the "SHELF" ♥ When the "class" of your DREAMS convenes, bypass any HINDRANCE to make sure that you are "in attendance". Avoid DETENTION by "showing up" and paying ATTENTION...and never risk your satisfaction's SUSPENSION. Do not make "excuses" for INACTION...There is no good "reason" to "POSTPONE" your PROSPERITY ♥You can "have-it-ALL" when you choose not to "STALL", so without "FURTHER ado", bring your PASSIONS to you! When it comes to your HOPES, "hammer away" without further DELAY...and make TODAY your "SOMEDAY" ♥ (LCF)

Lauren Christine Frahn

QUELL A QUARREL

♥ Do your best to EXTINGUISH arguments and certainly don't be the one to START them. There are much more EFFECTIVE ways of expressing yourself. CALMY CONVEY what you want to SAY and, if necessary, REMOVE yourself from the situation ♥ I am not suggesting to SURRENDER your BELIEFS if you KNOW yourself to be right...be FIRM in your CONVICTIONS... but understand that CONFLICT is not necessary in order to ACCOMPLISH this. Get your point across, as POLITELY as possible, and be done with it ♥ On the flip side, do not PROLONG an argument simply because you are too "proud" to ADMIT that you are wrong, for it is much NOBLER to DISPEL the tension with such an ACKNOWLEDGMENT ♥ If someone attempts to pick a FEUD with you, understand that the only way for it to PERPETUATE is if you PARTICIPATE...QUELL a QUARREL and promote PEACE, for most RESOLUTIONS are made in times of CALMNESS and CLARITY ♥ (LCF)

QUIET CONFIDENCE

♥ When you have CONFIDENCE, there is no need to make a "SPECTACLE" of it. If you believe in yourself, this CERTAINTY is certainly "APPARENT" to others **_without_** your needing to "ADVERTISE". True CONFIDENCE "speaks" for itself...let it do its job on its own ♥ Feeling the need to make a SHOWY "display" of "boldness" to others EXHIBITS that you likely do not possess the "PIZAZZ" that you are trying to PORTRAY. Having to SELF-DECLARE your "SPUNK" indicates that you doubt that your SURENESS shows, which means that you doubt yourself. In this case, your focus should not be on what others may perceive, but instead on finding a way to build UP your SELF-ESTEEM ♥ When you have TRUE FAITH in yourself, the best expression of this is actually UNEXPRESSED. The "secret" to being ADMIRED for your "FORTITUDE" lies in the "attitude" of keeping it a SECRET ♥ (LCF)

Lauren Christine Frahn

"Break free" from GLOOM by bringing forth the GLEAM of GLADNESS in others and in turn, create a BEACON of LIGHT for YOU to find your way back to" (LCF)

R.A.I.N. DROPS TO SUCCESS

♥ While the first RAINDROP in a bucket is hard to see, CONTINUAL rain will eventually FILL it to OVERFLOWING...The same is true of the ACTIONS you take to reach your DREAMS...Let them "POUR"! ♥ It is so important to view each and every EFFORT toward your goals as SIGNIFICANT, no matter how "SMALL"... it is these little "DROPLETS" of "precipitation" that will ACCUMULATE over time to bring you your "storm" of PROSPERITY. You will ARRIVE at your GOALS much QUICKER if you take these smaller actions CONSISTENTLY, versus waiting for the "BIG" move every "now and then" ♥ The LIGHT "DRIZZLE" of your actions will eventually bring the "DOWN-POUR" of your SUCCESS. As you "WEATHER" the journey to your DREAMS, always remember the "R.A.I.N"...Repeated Action is Necessary! ♥ (LCF)

Lauren Christine Frahn

RSVP "NO" TO TEMPTATION

♥ We are DRAWN to it...It exists ALL around us and makes its attempt to "LURE" us in EVERY chance that it can get! It has CONTROL over us ONLY when we ALLOW it. It is a powerful "SENSATION", which goes by the name of "TEMPTATION"! ♥ INSIST on your ability to RESIST its "call"...Rely on your WILL in order to DENY its "POWER". While it may feel easier to give in to its "ATTRACTION", really it serves as a "DISTRACTION" from your ultimate GOOD ♥ Often the "ALLURE" carries a circumstance that is "UNPURE"...your likeliness to be SEDUCED can be REDUCED by thinking of how much better you will FEEL once you REJECT its "APPEAL". When you RSVP "NO" to the "invitation" of PROVOCATION, you are saying "YES" to a much larger "CELEBRATION" in your HONOR!! ♥ (LCF)

RAINBOW OF GOOD CHEER

♥ PLEASURE should not be "put off" to some point in the FUTURE in anticipation of an "ideal" situation or event to take place. Realistically, this "date" that you are DELAYING your DELIGHT for may not even occur. HAPPINESS is not a "WHEN" ♥ If GOOD SPIRITS are ultimately what you are "seeking", stop "hiding" from them! You are surrounded by reasons to be happy RIGHT NOW...CHOOSE to see and feel the ENCHANTMENT that surrounds you. If you got out of bed this morning, right there is an extraordinary reason to be LIGHTHEARTED, for the greatest gift is that of a healthy heart providing you the BLESSING of another day ♥ HAPPINESS will bring you a WEALTH greater than ANY material possession...There is a "pot of gold" waiting for you EVERY day as long as you CHOOSE to discover the "rainbow" of GOOD CHEER... HAPPINESS HAPPENS BY CHOICE, NOT by CHANCE ♥ (LCF)

Lauren Christine Frahn

157

REACH FOR THE MOON, BUT GAZE AT THE STARS

♥ "All-ways" be on the "LOOKOUT" to IMPROVE your life in ALL possible WAYS, but make sure that you "SEE" what life ALREADY offers with the arrival of each of your days ♥ In your "hunt" to add more "loot" to your "chest of TREASURES", be "resolute" in your efforts to APPRECIATE the VALUE of "everyday" PLEASURES ♥ Every "minute" provides an opportunity to RECOGNIZE the BEAUTY that surrounds you, all that is required is your "GLANCE", so take the "TIME" to CHERISH each moment while you are "keeping WATCH" for ways to "advance" ♥ "Stay HUNGRY" for another "helping" while maintaining an "appetite" that is "well-deserving", but before asking for "SECONDS", make sure that you have "SAVORED" your FIRST "serving" ♥ "Go for the gold" when it comes to all that you "PRIZE" after, but do not forget that the greatest "AWARDS" are those of LOVE and LAUGHTER ♥ Only authentic GRATITUDE will bring you genuine PLENTITUDE. Never "discount" all of the "FORTUNES" that you currently MAINTAIN, or you will never be successful in pursuit of the ones that you have YET to "attain" ♥ REACH FOR THE MOON...But do not forget to GAZE at the STARS that already "TWINKLE" in your life ♥ (LCF)

Words Beneath Wings

RECIPE FOR SUCCESS

♥ There is no "magic potion" to create SUCCESS... It is a TIME-TESTED "recipe" made from basic ingredients that EACH of us POSSESS ♥ It all starts with an IDEA and when "MIXED" with the proper amounts of DETERMINATION, HARD WORK and PERSISTENCE, creates your "award-winning DISH" ♥ The amount of SUCCESS that you RECEIVE will be in DIRECT proportion to the amount of "SERVINGS" that you are willing to MAKE. If one "BATCH" comes out wrong and you "throw in the dish towel", you will not ACHIEVE the "DOZENS" more that you are more that you are CAPABLE of baking. However, should you CHOOSE to APPLY what you learned to the "next batch", it will be your BEST-TASTING yet, making each "BATTER" that follows better and BETTER! ♥ "BAKE" the "RECIPE" of your DREAMS with unconditional LOVE, for even when the "DOUGH" gets a little "sticky", throw in your "ALL-PURPOSE" flour...and "STICK" WITH IT! ♥ (LCF)

Lauren Christine Frahn

REMEDY FOR "SINGLEHOOD-ITIS"

♥ There is yet to be a "breakthrough drug" developed to cure "SINGLEHOOD-ITIS"...you know why? Because there's NOTHING wrong with you! ☺ ♥ There truly is someone "out there" for everyone. If you have yet to be struck by "CUPID'S ARROW", be PATIENT...there is a Power much greater than you that is TIMING everything in the PERFECT order so that you WILL FIND "that" person..."right on time" ♥ Do not search desperately with "rose-tinted" glasses, for this often leads to SETTLING...If you are going to settle, "settle into your OWN skin"...and find CONTENTMENT ♥ ENJOY YOU! I truly believe that if you fill YOURSELF with enough LOVE, you become much easier TO love. If you can't love yourself FIRST, how can you expect someone ELSE to? ♥ Remove yourself from any "clinical trials" and stop looking for a "prescription"...the only REMEDY you need is to RELAX...and ROMANCE YOURSELF! ;) ♥ (LCF)

"Your "colorful" REPUTATION does not mean much if the QUALITY of your DISPOSITION "pales" in comparison"

Lauren Christine Frahn

REMOVED UNTIL IMPROVED

♥ Be aware of your FEELINGS before any of your "DEALINGS"...If you are not at your BEST, give your interactions a temporary REST ♥ Take a bit of "DOWN-time" when feeling LOW in order to "pick yourself up" HIGH so that your ENCOUNTERS will always RAISE the spirits of both loved ones and passersby! ♥ You always want to leave a person feeling GREAT, so if you are not in a position to ELEVATE, than your "meeting" should surely WAIT. Do not get yourself into a "pickle" just because you are "FICKLE"! If a relationship has the potential to go a "LONG" way, do not allow a "SHORT-temper" to put a damper on this "headway" ♥ If you would prefer to be ALONE, this will surely come across in your "TONE", so don't "pick up the PHONE"! Remember, sometimes what you intend to CONVEY can come across a different WAY if your INFLECTION sends a signal in the "opposite DIRECTION"! Wait until your GOOD SPIRITS have replenished their "lack" before making a "callback"! ♥ Your goal should always be to make another feel BETTER, so take this into "con-sideration" before drafting an email or a LETTER. Be sure that the ENERGY that you write with does not create a "DETACHMENT" because whether you intend it or not, your MOOD will ALWAYS come through as an automatic "ATTACHMENT"! Eliminate FRUSTRATION from your mail's "translation" and guarantee that it only brings ELATION! ♥ If you are feeling "irriTA-BLE", do not sit down at a "table" with manners that will cause you to be CONTRITE...Excuse yourself and get a "breath of fresh air" until you are ready to be POLITE! ♥ Remember, it is best to pull an act of eva-sion rather than leave another with an "abrasion"... Never leave another "bruised" and "blue" as a result of your RENDEZVOUS! ♥ Take a bit of a DELAY until you are sure that you can BRIGHTEN another's DAY! Stay REMOVED until you feel that you have IMPROVED and get right back "in gear" when you are READY to bring CHEER! ♥ (LCF)

RESULTS "FROM CONCENTRATE"

♥ Trying to take on too many activities AT ONCE can DILUTE the effect of your actions…"HAND SELECT" your OBJECTIVES and make sure that your EFFORTS are "from CONCENTRATE" ♥ FOCUS your ENERGY on the goals that mean the most to you and PICK only the goals that are the most "RIPE" from the "TREE" of OPPORTUNITY ♥ In SQUEEZING out ALL that you can from the "FRUIT" of EACH PURSUIT, you will be "filling your cup" with the juices of SUCCESS and GRATIFICATION ♥ PRIORITIZE your ASPIRATIONS, so as not to put a STRAIN on the amount of "PULP" that you can PRODUCE ♥ (LCF)

S.O.S.!

♥ In order to draw SUCCESS "near", you must not REPEL it with thoughts of FEAR ♥ Figure out the "nitty-gritty" of what truly MATTERS to you...without paying attention to ITTY-BITTY "matters" ♥ Once you determine your heart's "burning" DESIRE, throw any sources of SELF-DOUBT into its "FIRE" ♥ Your GOALS will only SURVIVE in your "SUNLIGHT"...STRIVE to keep them ALIVE and BRIGHT by removing them from the "darkness" of FRIGHT ♥ For PROSPERITY to come, apply this LCF "rule of thumb": "NEGATIVITY REPELS and POSITIVITY PROPELS"! ♥ "KNUCKLE DOWN" on your task "at HAND" and release the "GRIP" on your GRIPES! ♥ Keep your eyes AHEAD...and never "look back" with DREAD. In order to keep your "sights set" on the STARS, you cannot be "gazing" at past SCARS! ♥ Keep your ASPIRATIONS "AFLOAT" by not "drowning" yourself with signals of DISTRESS. If you send out an "S.O.S.!" action, be sure that it "reflects" your "Sights. On. Satisfaction.!" ♥ Giving "notoriety" to thoughts of ANXIETY will create a "mirage" of DISABILITY...DISEMPOWER this "illusion" with perceptions of POSSIBILITY! ♥ Put ATTRACTIVE "visions" in your "SPOTLIGHT" so that DETRACTIVE images do

Lauren Christine Frahn

165

not "shadow" your PLIGHT ♥ Set your SIGHTS strictly on the FINISH LINE...and never WORRY that you will have to "resign" ♥ "ZERO IN" on your "target" with "zero" MISGIVING for the BEST possible life that you are capable of LIVING! ♥ "Hunger" for HAPPINESS and never allow FRIGHT to curb this "appetite"! Continually SATISFY your "craving" for WELL-BEING... and "serve" your GREATER GOOD ♥ (LCF)

SCARY GOOD SUCCESS

♥ On the way to your DREAMS, it is expected that FRIGHT will appear "in SIGHT"...it simply means that you have a great "line of VISION"! Throughout these ADVENTURES to your ENDEAVORS, allow EXCITATION to overpower any TREPIDATION...you are only "IN GEAR" when you have a little bit of FEAR! ♥ The ideal "recipe" for a GOAL involves "heaping" measures of MANIC with only a few "shakes" of PANIC...Stir in SUCCESS with only a "pinch" of added STRESS for a "dish" that is sure to IMPRESS! ♥ View your AMBITIONS as more of a "DELIGHT" than a "PLIGHT"! ♥ It is perfectly "normal" to have feelings of HESITATION when it comes to an ASPIRATION... Simply shift your CONCENTRATION to the end result of JUBILATION to achieve "out-of-this-world" results! ♥ Do not FRET over a CRAVING's "COLD SWEAT", but feel the "HEAT" of your FEAT'S "FEVER" ♥ "Ignite" your WILL by focusing on the THRILL...and instantly "warm up" your COLD FEET ♥ Do not allow DREAD to "mess" with your head..."Clean up" your BRAIN with THRILLING thoughts of ALL that you will ATTAIN! ♥ Do not get caught up in HYSTERIA and permit WOE to "WORRY-ya"! Remember, some feelings of DISMAY are "OKAY"...you are ON YOUR WAY to your "GLORY DAY"! ♥ View your fear as a "SCARE TACTIC", designed strictly to force your steps toward your "FANTASTIC"! ♥ (LCF)

Lauren Christine Frahn

SCRUTINIZE BEFORE YOU VERBALIZE

♥ SCRUTINIZE before you VERBALIZE and only COMMUNICATE when your CONTEXT is CORDIAL ♥ WORDS carry tremendous "POWER" and MEANING... make sure they are "charged" with POSITIVE "energy" and never DEMEANING ♥ You do not "afford" the right to speak in JEST at another's "expense" just because you may not be feeling at your BEST. Work on "elevat-ing" yourself to a "HIGHER" MOOD before UTTERING a statement that will be considered "rude" ♥ A THOUGHT always precedes what you SPEAK ~ If it is not a THOUGHTFUL one, "refrain" from uttering the "disdain". It is always your CHOICE what it is that you decide to VOICE. When someone carries you to your "brink", take a second to THINK...As soon as you realize this urge to VOCALIZE something "hateful", bring to mind all of the reasons that you are GRATEFUL ♥ Before you "deliver" DIALECT that will send one's feelings "south", remember that there is no "BACKSPACE" on the "keyboard" of your MOUTH. You can never "reverse" something that you CONVERSE ♥ Before you "BREAK the silence", be sure that you do not do the same to someone's heart, spirit, or dreams. Always make your words the WIND beneath one's WINGS and you, in turn, will SOAR ♥ (LCF)

Words Beneath Wings

SET THE TABLE FOR YOUR DAY

♥ Provide good "DIRECTION" for your day by "CHANNELING" all thoughts to "GO YOUR WAY" ♥ Every morning, "SET THE TABLE" for the "course" of the day by IMAGINING it to be the very best "BANQUET" that you have ever attended...Use only the FINEST "silverware" and lay each "dish" with "INTENTION" and "CARE" ♥ "CALCULATE" the "numerous" events of the day ahead of time, using your mind's POSITIVE "powers"...and "COUNT ON" a terrific "24 HOURS" ♥ "FORECAST" nothing but "sunny skies" for the day by chasing away any "clouds" of doubt that would make it "overcast" ♥ "IRON OUT" the events of the day in your mind...and see them "unfolding" without a "wrinkle" or a "crease" ♥ "BARGAIN ON" the greatest of "transactions" throughout the day by forcing the "liquidation" of all thoughts that would "cost" you from "sealing this deal" ♥ "ANTICIPATE" both giving and receiving the highest of REGARDS, "BELIEVING" that in whatever the day "deals" you, a "royal flush" is "IN THE CARDS" ♥ When you CHOOSE to "FORESEE" total "GLEE", your life will "display" before your eyes "accordin-glee"..."CONTEMPLATE" the "FATE" of this "DATE" with thoughts that are "GREAT"! ♥ (LCF)

Lauren Christine Frahn

SHARE THE WEALTH

♥ It is wonderful to be AMBITIOUS and to strive for SUCCESS, but if you are doing it simply to see how many POSSESSIONS you can ACCUMULATE or how much money that can add up in your bank account... really, what is the point? ♥ What is the point of living in the lap of LUXURY if there is no one there to sit on YOUR lap? If you are not SHARING and ENJOYING your BELONGINGS with others, you are eventually going to "long" for a place TO belong ♥ Don't get me wrong, there is nothing wrong with trying to accumulate REVENUE and ABUNDANCE...we are all meant to live such lives...but you must not forget that you cannot take it with you when you go...SHARE and SPREAD your WEALTH with others. If you take a second to think about the greatest moments in your life, I am quite certain that the majority of them have NOTHING to do with WHAT you OWNED, but rather WHOM you were WITH. Life is so much more REWARDING when "amassing rewards" is not your life ♥ If you focus SOLELY on the ACCUMULATION of your ASSETS, this process will eventually be your greatest LIABILITY ♥ Use your AFFLUENCE to positively INFLUENCE others and promote GOOD with your GOOD FORTUNE...When you use your TREASURE to bring PLEASURE to others, that is the BEAUTY of TRUE WEALTH ♥ (LCF)

Words Beneath Wings

SILENCE THE CRITICS

♥ Regardless of how AMAZING you are, chances are that you will encounter CRITICS who like to offer you their "OPINION"...Be comfortable enough in your OWN flesh, so as not to let any of them get "under your skin". Focus on ALL of those that LOVE and SUPPORT you, not on the very FEW that do not ♥ CRITICISM can only hurt if you allow yourself to be reached by the cold, verbal "STICKS and STONES"...Ward them off by concentrating, instead, on those who "stone-cold" STICK BY you. Please do not allow fear of a verbal ASSAULT to be a BLOCKADE that you stand BEHIND, but allow the SUPPORT of those who STAND BEHIND YOU to continue to PROPEL you FORWARD. Take COURAGE in those who ENCOURAGE you ♥ When NEGATIVITY comes your way, have zero REMORSE... there are plenty MORE that 100% ENDORSE you ♥ The only way that INSULTS can get the best of you is if you permit them to..."Drown out" the SNEERS and JEERS with the much louder CHEERS...and SILENCE THE CRITICS ♥ (LCF)

Lauren Christine Frahn

171

"Get caught up in your MOMENTS...these TEMPORARY twinkles of time are as dazzling and unique as snow-flakes, but also just as VANISHING. Do not let them FADE without your ACCOLADE"

Words Beneath *Wings*

SNOWFLAKE MOMENTS

♥ Get caught up in your MOMENTS. These TEMPORARY "twinkles" of time are as dazzling and unique as SNOWFLAKES, but also just as VANISHING... Do not let them "FADE" without your "ACCOLADE" ♥ Take the TIME to SEE the beauty of each SECOND, for there is no "second" CHANCE if you let one pass without a GLANCE. A clock's hand will continue to "TICK" no matter how hard you try to make the minute "STICK" ♥ Each "GEM" of time is PRECIOUS, for its "display" is SHORT-LIVED...and when the moment doesn't exactly "SPARKLE", this very "quality" of TRANSIENCE is where the VALUE lies...Find the BEAUTY here in the fact that it will PASS ♥ When striving for a WIN, but come up with an occasional "FAIL", keep your head up knowing that this occasion's "SHIP" will "SAIL" ♥ APPRECIATE each "DATE" and don't show up late... for even if you look extra "spiffy", they'll be gone in a "JIFFY"! On the contrary, if one happens to arrive with an "unfriendly GREETING", relax in knowing that its visit is "FLEETING"! ♥ (LCF)

Lauren Christine Frahn

173

SPECTACLES OF SUCCESS

♥ If you don't "PERCEIVE" yourself as an "ACHIEVER", it is impossible to PERFORM as one...It is only when you "CONCEIVE" yourself to be a PERSON OF ACTION that you can actually become one ♥ In order to create an "ELECTRIFYING" life, you must first IMAGINE yourself as a "LIGHTNING ROD" in order to "CONDUCT" your behavior accordingly. The SKY is the limit for you so long as you REGARD yourself as the "RISING STAR" that you are! ♥ When you BELIEVE that your efforts are "WORTH-while" and can ENVISION yourself as having tremendous "VALUE", you will produce RESULTS of equal "WORTH". As soon as you "RECOGNIZE" yourself as being capable of ANYTHING, you can "REALIZE" EVERYTHING that you "VISUALIZE"! ♥ Eliminate your "SHORT-SIGHTED" outlook by always wearing your "SPECTACLES" of SUCCESS...the VIEW will become nothing "short" of "SPECTACULAR"!!♥ (LCF)

START WITH NUMBER ONE

♥ In order to give your BEST to OTHERS, you must first give your BEST to YOURSELF. It is impossible to be able to TEND to the needs of another when YOUR needs are UNATTENDED to. There is a MISCONCEPTION that putting YOU first can be an act of selfishness, however, when you DEPRIVE yourself of DEVOTION, you have nothing to DEVOTE to your loved ones. PAMPER yourself so as not to put a DAMPER on the SPOILS that you could PROVIDE to others ♥ ABUNDANCE of self allows for the reward of INDULGENCE to others. Understand that it is only by servicing yourself FIRST that you can be OF SERVICE to those around you. TAKE COMFORT in the fact that by comforting yourself, you are able to comfort others. You can only ENRICH the life of another when you have met your own ESSENTIAL requirements. The CHANCE to ENHANCE another begins when you begin by ALLOTTING a LOT of LOVE to Y-O-U. Hold yourself accountable for your own WELL-BEING by not refusing your own REPLENISHMENT ♥ Count on this...In order to get to number two, you have to start with NUMBER ONE ♥ (LCF)

Lauren Christine Frahn

STAY THE COURSE

♥ The "ASPHALT" on your "ASPIRATION SUPERHIGHWAY" will not always be "SMOOTH", but in order to SUCCEED, you must hurdle any of the "BUMPS" that come your way. The only one that can "turn" these temporary "ROADBLOCKS" into permanent "BLOCKADES" is you... Do not make a "U-TURN"! ♥ Even if you have been meaning-LESSly staring at the same "HIGHWAY POST" for a significant period of time due to an "OBSTRUCTION" ahead, look for the "meaning-FULL" "SIGN"! Even with SETBACKS, there is OPPORTUNITY...in fact, every setback IS an opportunity! Each IMPEDIMENT provides a LESSON that will put you on an even smoother "ROADWAY" to SUCCESS and bring you one "MILE-MARKER" closer to your ultimate "DESTINATION" ♥ When you APPLY what you LEARN from every "BARRICADE", you are "PAVING" the "road" ahead to the "LOCATION" of your DREAMS ♥ FAILURES are not "DEAD-ENDS". Where there is MOTIVATION and "DRIVE", there is always a WAY...STAY THE COURSE ♥ (LCF)

STEREOTYPE STATIC

♥ It is impossible to experience the HARMONIES of all of the many different kinds of MUSIC if you keep yourself LIMITED to listening only to your PRESET stations. In the same manner, do not place a LIMIT on the VARIETY of beautiful EXPERIENCES that you may have with others based on your PRE-ORDAINED STEREOTYPES ♥ "Turn the dial" of your thought process away from the network of "PREDETERMINED OPINION" and TUNE in to another's TRUE FREQUENCY... You will likely discover a whole NEW GENRE that you LOVE! Remember this before AUTOMATICALLY going to your "PRESETS" in all of your INTERACTIONS on a daily basis ♥ "Change the channels" in your mind from ones that are PRE-PROGRAMMED to those of RECEPTIVITY, for you must first LISTEN to the SOUNDS of the songs BEFORE you decide your STANCE ♥ Don't let the "STATIC of STEREOTYPE" interfere with music's MELODIOUS UNDERTONES, for you will prevent your-self from HEARING perhaps the most WONDERFUL "LYRICS" that you ever listened to ♥ (LCF)

Lauren Christine Frahn

STICK TO YOUR JOB DESCRIPTION

♥ When it comes to GOAL FORMATION for your LIFE, stay within your CAREER "description"! Stick to your area of EXPERTISE, which involves figuring out the "WHAT". Be very PRECISE and EXACT regarding WHAT it is that you want to ACHIEVE...and BELIEVE that you have the ABILITY to ACCOMPLISH it! For now, your JOB is complete...The "HOW" will be MANAGED by a much "Higher Authority" ♥ Trying to figure out HOW you will accomplish every detail will just SLOW DOWN the process of bringing you what you WANT...regardless of how intelligent you are, there is a FORCE much smarter than you "AT WORK" ♥ Once shown "the way", you will know you are on the FAST TRACK for a LIFE "PROMOTION" as long your work doesn't feel like a tedious "TASK". When you are being DIVINELY guided, your ACTIONS will seem more LEISURE than LABOR ♥ Avoid "termination" by trying to PERFORM the JOB of a SUPERIOR. Make your INTENTION and then pay ATTENTION, for it is GOD who will PROD you to ACTION ♥ (LCF)

STICKS & STONES

♥ If someone throws "STICKS and STONES", all they can break are your bones...Your SPIRIT should remain "in tact" despite any verbal "ATTACK" ♥ Always stay true to Y-O-U...If NEGATIVITY is "HURLED" in your direction, never change YOUR direction for what you want in life. You must not allow another's WORDS to "CRUSH" your SELF-ESTEEM or permit one's "CHEAP SHOT" to "cheapen" your SELF-WORTH! No matter who tries to "BLACK EYE" your HOPES or DREAMS, keep your "blinders on" with the VISION of your GOAL clear in SIGHT ♥ It is difficult to hear CRITICISM, but you can "SHOVE" away the DEFAMATION by "LAUNCHING" it into an AFFIRMATION! Remind yourself of ALL of the reasons that you are so SPECIAL on a daily basis and create a "SHIELD" of CONFIDENCE that no "PUT-DOWN" can "penetrate!" ♥ When you are struck with a SLANDER "DART", keep a SMILE in your HEART and RECHARGE your "battery" with self FLATTERY. The next time someone delivers you a "SLAP IN THE FACE", maintain your GRACE...and KEEP YOUR PACE ♥ (LCF)

Lauren Christine Frahn

179

STRIKING MOMENTS
DEFINE YOU

♥ There may be times in life where it feels that a METEOR has suddenly STRUCK everything that you knew to be "normal" and sent it flying into the air. LET THE PIECES GO... ♥ Do not frantically attempt to grab the debris from space, for you will be interrupting one of the most AMAZING processes that we as humans face. WHO we presently ARE has been shaped by EACH and EVERY experience and encounter that we have ever had ♥ While you may feel completely OUT OF control, understand that what is happening is Divinely UNDER CONTROL. When life delivers a BOOM, it is simply making ROOM for a newly formed TRAIT predestined by your FATE ♥ There are absolutely NO MISTAKES in what these QUAKES shake into our lives. Allow the dust to SETTLE where it may, revealing in its AFTERMATH the BEAUTY of something much larger than us at work. It is these STRIKING moments that have the greatest IMPACT on who we are...ultimately, they are what DEFINES us ♥ (LCF)

SUCCESS AS YOUR SHADOW

♥ Avoid making an "empty" career start by choosing something that fills your HEART. "Lead" with what you LOVE to do and the REWARD will "follow" you ♥ Before you decide on an OCCUPATION, be sure that your motive is coming from the proper "location". When you "start" a JOB as a means to a DOLLAR SIGN "end", the experience of DISSATISFACTION is something with which you will not be able to "contend". In basing your decision on something "below" what your SOUL would have "willed", you are making the chances quite HIGH that you will not be FULFILLED ♥ Question yourself as to what you would CHOOSE if there was no possibility for you to LOSE and take ACTION based on this very REACTION...What it is that you REMARK is the "starting point" from which your DEEPEST DREAMS should "embark" ♥ If your "STEPS" forward are taken in pursing your true PASSION, SUCCESS will be your "SHADOW" ♥ (LCF)

""ALL-WAYS" be OPEN-MINDED to opportunity...and "forevermore" be SUSCEPTIBLE to INCREDIBLE"

SUSCEPTIBLE TO INCREDIBLE

♥ Wherever there is HUMANITY, there is POSSIBILITY... containing the ABILITY to transform your life...BE OPEN to the CHANGE ♥ Keep an OPEN MIND to a "novel" IDEA or NOTION, so as not to CLOSE the "book" on what the Universe has put in MOTION. Always be "ALERT" to POSSIBILITIES for MORE, so as never to "slam" OPPORTUNITY'S "DOOR" ♥ Continually WELCOME new suggestions...while some of these "ingestions" may be "hard to swallow", they may be just what you need to feel BETTER TOMORROW ♥ PAY ATTENTION to "strangers" who cross your path, remembering that the Universe has a "familiar" PERFECTION of bring- ing the right people together in the most wonder- ful of ways...be APPROACHABLE by these PROSPECTS throughout each and every one of your days ♥ Open the "EYES" of your HEART...and be on the LOOKOUT for all of the affection that the world is looking to IMPART. If searching for LOVE, be RECEPTIVE to find- ing it...Give your heart to FATE and remember, your next encounter could be your LAST "FIRST" DATE ♥ ACCEPT any INVITATION with EXCITATION, for it may just put your "Life's a Beach" WITHIN REACH! ♥ Make no mistake that everything you HEAR is the Universe

Lauren Christine Frahn

"at PLAY", so always TUNE IN to what others have to SAY...What you "get wind of" could be the very "gust" that whisks you away to your "everyday holiday"! Be "ALL EARS" to both strangers and peers...You never know whose VOICE will make "Life's a BREEZE" your slogan of CHOICE! ♥ "ALL-WAYS" be OPEN-MINDED... and "forevermore" be SUSCEPTIBLE to INCREDIBLE ♥ (LCF)

SUSTAIN YOUR GAIN

♥ The "actualization" of your GOALS does not guarantee their automatic "continuation" ♥ The "GAIN" that you "ATTAIN" will only "REMAIN" if you do what it takes to "SUSTAIN" it. You must apply your "DEXTERITY" each and every DAY if you wish "PROSPERITY" to STAY ♥ Do not make the "assumption" that your continued "GUMPTION" is "UNESSENTIAL", for this "PRESUMPTION" will serve to severely limit your POTENTIAL. Always keep your "shift" in HIGH GEAR, so as not to become NEUTRAL in your "DRIVE". Keep your "fire burning", so as not to become "LUKEWARM" in the "heat" of your "PASSIONS" ♥ Your "PROGRESS" will be "momentary" if you permit your "MOMENT-um" to "regress". Maintain a "tight grip" on your ultimate "OBJECTIVES", so as not to become "DETACHED" from these ideal "ELECTIVES" ♥ Your "days" will start to "lack" if you become "LACKADAISICAL". If the "taste" of SUCCESS is something you want to continue to "SAVOR", you must put in the required "LABOR" ♥ Meet your ACHIEVEMENT with an "EMBRACEMENT", but then do not become "COMPLACENT"...Allow yourself feelings of "well-DESERVED" "PRIDE", but do not then

Lauren Christine Frahn

become "RESERVED" in your "STRIDE" ♥ When you get to eye-level with the "bar" that you have set, the time has come to RAISE IT further yet. In the "competition" of LIFE, always continue to "go for the gold medal"...and NEVER SETTLE! ♥

SWEET vs. SUBMISSIVE

♥ There is a major difference between being SWEET and being SUBMISSIVE...It is one thing to always be as GIVING as possible, but quite another to always be "GIVING IN". Do not lose your ADVANTAGE by allowing yourself to be TAKEN ADVANTAGE OF ♥ RESPECT yourself by refusing another's attempt to show you DISPRESPECT. Do not be afraid to "use your BACKBONE" and STAND UP for yourself...you can SPEAK your mind, without being OUTSPOKEN ♥ Stand your GROUND, so as to never get BACKED into a corner. It is NOT "okay" to permit someone to "WALK all over you", let alone leave even a SINGLE footprint... that is what DOORMATS are for...and I assure you that YOU are NOT one of them ♥ Your WORTH is tremendous...never cheapen your VALUE for one who does not value YOU. "Bend over backwards" only when you are braced...and EMBRACED ♥ (LCF)

SWING, BATTER, SWING!

♥ "STEP UP TO THE PLATE" to make the most of your "FATE" ♥ When life throws the occasional "curve ball", are you going to NOT REACT?... or will you do your best to MAKE CONTACT?! As soon as you notice that the path is "ASKEW", remember that the very next MOVE is up to Y-O-U ♥ While you do not have CONTROL as to when a "WILD PITCH" is "hurled" your way, it is up to YOU to DECIDE the "STRATEGY" with which you are going to "PLAY" ♥ Assume "RESPONSIBILITY" by responding with "AGILITY"... There is no room in the "batter's box" for BLAME, so it is up to YOU to keep your HEAD "IN THE GAME" ♥ Always keep your "EYES OPEN", but never get "caught looking". When you maintain a "GOOD EYE", this "eye-opening" experience will not be able to catch you "off guard" ♥ A "STRIKE-OUT" is only a guarantee if you give the "ball" a "ONCE-OVER"..."once" it is "OVER" the plate. Instead of a mere "glance", CHOOSE to make the very BEST of this "launch" by adjusting your "STANCE" ♥ Keep your focus on the MOUND and PREPARE for the cheers to "resound"...GET SET for the "BALL" and use your "POWER" to send it "OVER THE WALL"! When "THROWN for a loop", make the very best of the "FLING"...and "SWING, BATTER, SWING!" ♥ (LCF)

SYMPHONY OF "MISTAKES"

♥ Don't "mistake" a MISTAKE as something NEGATIVE..."LISTEN UP" for the POSITIVE message that it is delivering to you. It is these very LESSONS that will teach you the "KEYS" to get you in better HARMONY with your ultimate GOALS and VISIONS ♥ GET "IN TUNE" with the OPPORTUNITIES provided to you in "off-key" experiences. When you learn the new "NOTES" that you have been presented with, you will be able to "COMPOSE" the best possible "MUSIC" of your life ♥ Stay VERSED in the lessons learned and APPLY them to every new "piece" that you COMPOSE so that the ECHOES of PAST "notes" of DISCORD do not RESOUND. By making sure to NOT REPEAT any of your previous "off-key" LYRICS, you put yourself "on TEMPO" for creating the most amazing SYMPHONY of your life ♥ (LCF)

Lauren Christine Frahn

TAKE YOUR "FREE-WAY" TO SUCCESS

♥ If you FOLLOW, follow only for GUIDANCE, but strive to LEAD YOUR OWN WAY ♥ Be sure that the person that puts you "in tow" will STEER you in the RIGHT DIRECTION and bears a "TITLE" that only ENHANCES your VALUE ♥ TAKE GOOD DIRECTION, but only until you see the "RAMP" to the "HIGHWAY" of your OWN dreams... "UNHITCH" yourself and get on the "FREE-WAY" toward your ultimate SUCCESS ♥ Always "take the HIGH ROAD"...As you LEAD, lead by good EXAMPLE. Do not "cut anyone off" in order to "GAIN MILEAGE", for the only thing that you should "BURN" is some "RUBBER"! ♥ Follow your OWN "MAP" and stay in your OWN "LANE"...just make sure that your are not getting "PASSED" on any side ;) ♥ (LCF)

T.A.S.T.E.

♥ ACTION on pure EMOTION can often cause undesired OVERREACTION in a situation ♥ When OVERWHELMED with a strong feeling, it seems "automatic" to act on IMPULSE, but this action ultimately may not serve your HIGHEST GOOD or the good of those involved ♥ PAUSE for a minute to determine if your words or actions will truly produce the DESIRED RESULT that you want, and then PROCEED ACCORDINGLY...While this requires intentional EFFORT at first, once "SEASONED" to it, it becomes second nature ♥ "SIMMER" your REACTION before it "BOILS OVER" by determining your thoughts and changing them for the BETTER. Doing so will change your FEELINGS and therefore, your RESPONSES, which will ultimately IMPROVE your overall circumstances in life ♥ "Sprinkle SUGAR" on your life and the lives of those around you without the harsh "SPICE" of HASTE by always remembering to "T.A.S.T.E.".."Take. A. Second. To. Evaluate." the FLAVOR of the situation before adding unnecessary "SALT" ♥ (LCF)

Lauren Christine Frahn

THE "F" WORD

♥ Pardon my language, but I need to use the "F" WORD! Yes, we are all guilty of it...FLAWS! ♥ It doesn't matter WHO you are, EVERYONE has something that they are not FOND of about themselves, but why FOCUS on THAT? What about ALL of the things that are FANTASTIC?? ♥ Switching from a "PROFANITY" to a POLITE request, PLEASE do not BEAT yourself up, but BUILD yourself up! You have SO many reasons that make you WORTHY of FAVOR! ♥ If you get the "F" WORD urge when looking in the mirror, REMOVE the self-criticism, MOVE your attention to a FAVORITE FEATURE...and FLAUNT it!! If it is a PERSONALITY trait or an ACTION that you performed, DO SOMETHING to CHANGE...and FIX it! CLEAN UP your "vocabulary" and EXPEL this "Expletive" from your life by focusing on all that you EXCEL in! ♥ It is time to realize that you are BECOMING...and become your OWN biggest FAN! When on the verge of the "F" WORD, take a second to turn it into a POSITIVE, for you are FABULOUS! ♥ (LCF)

THE "OTHER" GOLDEN RULE

♥ While the "GOLDEN RULE" reigns SUPREME, you must also hold YOURSELF in ESTEEM ♥ There is a direct CORRELATION between how you treat YOURSELF and how OTHERS treat YOU...it is absolute FACT that, in this "relationship", OPPOSITES do NOT "ATTRACT"! ♥ REPRESENT yourself in a way that is REPRESENTATIVE of the way that you would like others to PRESENT themselves to you. You cannot "expect" RESPECT without SELF-RESPECT ♥ "SING A TUNE" that you would like others to "HARMONIZE" with ♥ "EXHIBIT" a "DISPLAY" that you would like others to ADMIRE ♥ "SHOWER" yourself with "SUNSHINE" if you do not want others to "RAIN" on your "parade" ♥ "ASSUME THE ROLE" of NOBILITY and "PLAY THE PART" of PRESTIGE if you wish others to REGARD your "CHARACTER" ♥ If your feelings are "FRAGILE", "HANDLE YOURSELF WITH CARE" so that others will treat you "DELICATELY" ♥ "CALL THE SHOTS" as to how others "take aim" at you by "TARGETING" your efforts to always SALUTE yourself with HONOR. Do not "SHOOT yourself in the foot" by failing to "put your BEST foot forward" when you CARRY YOURSELF ♥ REGARD yourself with REVERENCE...and "SYMBOLIZE" what you "IDEALIZE" ♥ (LCF)

Lauren Christine Frahn

THE PAST HAS PASSED

♥ No matter how hard you try, there is no way to change your "days gone by"...Let go of the PAST, for it has "PASSED" ♥ CHANGE the focus of any questioning from a woeful "WHY?" to an OPTIMISTIC "HOW?!"... and make your "impending" time "IMPECCABLE", using only your "HERE AND NOW" ♥ Even if you have received many "gifts" to-date that you wish you could have "exchanged", the current "PRESENT" is the only thing that makes a difference...because it is where YOU can MAKE a DIFFERENCE ♥ Your TOMORROW is created TODAY...not yesterday. If you are unhappy "at this MOMENT", take one to deter- mine if you have truly made the most of the ones that have already ELAPSED. The countdown for the "grand finale" of your FUTURE begins RIGHT NOW...are you lining up "FIREWORKS"?, or throwing your ability to do great "WORKS" into the "FIRE?? ♥ Remember, the only one that has to "pay" for carrying extra "bag- gage" is you..."Free" yourself to "FLY" by leaving that "luggage" BEHIND! ♥ When it comes to what is "YET TO COME", when you decide to choose HOPE, nothing is "IM-POSSIBLE"...Steal away this "I"-"M" attitude... and make everything POSSIBLE ♥ (LCF)

TIGHTEN THE "LOOSE SCREWS"

♥ If something doesn't feel right in your life, FIX IT... The reason that you have this "urge" to IMPLEMENT a CHANGE is because you are not currently in the state of HAPPINESS and CONTENTMENT that you are INTENDED to be ♥ HAMMER away at your HOPES instead of sitting with the WOBBLY feelings of UNSTEADINESS ♥ You are being ENLIGHTENED with the REVELATION that you have some "loose screws" that need to be TIGHTENED. When this light is SHED upon you, head to your inner TOOLSHED and get to WORK...All of the DEVICES necessary to make the needed ADJUSTMENTS are WITHIN you ♥ Do not "screw" around with the DRIVE that has been placed within you, but be the "SCREW-DRIVER" to your GOALS and twist away until they are LOCKED in place ♥ You are the MACHINE that can MEND whatever it is in your life that needs REPAIR...RESTORE yourself to OPTIMAL condition.   Never settle for a FRAGILE future...your DREAMS are not meant to be BROKEN ♥ (LCF)

Lauren Christine Frahn

TODAY

♥ If you've been waiting to start something new because you are allowing excuses to get in the WAY... start TODAY ♥ If you have been "all business" and have allowed yourself no time for PLAY...have some fun TODAY ♥ If you have kept yourself under a cloud of despair without any fresh air or SUNRAY...get outside TODAY ♥ If you've been putting off telling someone that you love him or her because you are not exactly sure what you want to SAY...make that call TODAY ♥ If you have been hurt in the past and have decided to push all love AWAY...let someone in TODAY ♥ If something has caused you to turn away from your faith and you no longer take the time to PRAY... talk to God TODAY ♥ If you have wandered from the person that you strive to be and now your hope is also ASTRAY...find yourself TODAY ♥ If something in your life is causing you worry and strife, trust and know that everything will truly be OKAY...exhale...and let it go TODAY ♥ If you have been trying so hard to control all of the events of your life, allow the Universe's "chips" to fall where they MAY... leave it all up to God, starting TODAY ♥ Without any further DELAY, make TODAY YOUR DAY...and do this EVERY DAY ♥ (LCF)

Words Beneath Wings

"Eliminate your SHORT-SIGHTED outlook by always wearing your SPECTACLES of SUCCESS...the VIEW will become nothing short of SPECTACULAR" (LCF)

Lauren Christine Frahn

"TODAY IS YOUR DAY"

♥ LIFE is not a "coming soon" ATTRACTION to be anticipated and enjoyed at some FUTURE date...the most recent BLOCKBUSTER release, "TODAY IS YOUR DAY", is the greatest "MOTION PICTURE" you will ever see...and it's LIVE, "starring" Y-O-U! ♥ Be sure that you are not "FAST-FORWARDING" through your life, for there is no way to ever "REWIND" it...Hit your "PAUSE button" and RELISH the PRESENT moments ♥ The BLESSINGS of TODAY are not meant to be "RECORDED" in order to watch and enjoy at some point "down the road" when you "make the time" to do so. The time is NOW..."TODAY IS YOUR DAY"...Hit PLAY! ♥

TRUE COLORS OF ANOTHER

♥ Never "close your eyes" to one's TRUE COLORS even if their current state is DULLING their normal SHINE ♥ At one point or another, for one reason or another, one's true colors sometimes get "BLOCKED", reflecting off SHADES that are NOT representative of his or her "true UNDERTONE"...look BENEATH this temporarily "tinted" COMPLEXION. Just because one's color may occasionally become MUTED does not mean that he or she will forever be LACKLUSTER ♥ Do your very best not to join them on their "end of the SPECTRUM" by passing judgment or holding this against them. Avoid casting off the same PALLID tones and instead, AIM to RESTORE their RADIANCE...use your VIBRANCY to help bring them back to a BRIGHTER "wavelength" ♥ While color is based on PERCEPTION, do not allow a moment of "GRAY" or "BLUE" to change your perception of another's "TRUE HUE" ♥ (LCF)

Lauren Christine Frahn

TUNE OUT NEGATIVITY

♥ Your brain can not determine the difference between what is REAL and what you REPEATEDLY "PICTURE" in your mind ♥ The majority of what the MEDIA broadcasts is NEGATIVITY because that is what grabs the ATTENTION of most! If you are "TUNING IN" to these programs that speak of negative SITUATIONS and portray negative EVENTS, your natural reaction when you "picture" these events in your mind is to give back feelings of...you guessed it... NEGATIVITY! The issue that occurs here is that some form of this negativity will eventually APPEAR in the "reality show" that is your LIFE, for what you "FEEL about", you will "BRING about" ♥ SURROUND yourself with only SOUNDS of POSITIVITY and be AWARE of what you CHOOSE to LISTEN TO and VIEW ♥ Be careful what you "tune into"...and perhaps, "TUNE OUT"! ♥ (LCF)

UNANSWERED PRAYERS

♥ Never lose HOPE when God does not seem to REPLY to your REQUESTS, for it simply means that He is working on something even BETTER♥ You are never "ignored" by the Lord...If you are awaiting an ANSWER posed from a "place" of "GRACE", just be PATIENT and TRUST in His eventual and perfect "EMBRACE". Do not let your SPIRITS get "DIMINISHED"...the master-piece of His RESPONSE is simply "UNFINISHED" ♥ It is SO important that you do not doubt your ABILITIES because, in NOT responding, God is showing you that He has COMPLETE FAITH in them ♥ When you are "on your KNEES", have patience in knowing that God will "APPEASE" your PENDING "PLEAS" in a way that "EXCEEDS" even your loftiest of "NEEDS". When a PRAYER is still "UP IN THE AIR", keep your EYES pointed in the same direction...I promise that it did not "FALL on deaf EARS" ♥ (LCF)

Lauren Christine Frahn

UPRIGHT MIGHT
MEAN UPHILL

♥ The CREDITABLE thing to do can also be the most CHALLENGING, but that is no EXCUSE to opt for the "EASY way out"...While easier said than done, once DONE, it is much EASIER to hold your head up HIGH ♥ It is crucial to make RIGHTEOUS decisions, regardless of whether they are the most RIGOROUS. It is these actions that become HABIT and ultimately, are what DEFINES you. The COMMENDABLE course of action might be the most DEMANDING, but VIRTUE demands these HARD-WON efforts ♥ Determine to do what is UPRIGHT, even if an UPHILL battle ♥ While it is true that what is WORTHY may be the most WEARISOME, it assuredly involves much less WEIGHT than that of the GUILT from choosing the "piece of cake" option ♥ Even if it is no picnic or walk in the park...regardless of the PRESSURE that may be involved...you have the POWER to always do what is PRAISEWORTHY ♥ (LCF)

VAULT OF TRUST

♥ There is SACREDNESS in having the HONOR of being ENTRUSTED with information by another. Being REVERED as someone who deserves this type of FAITH involves CONFIDENCE in the INTEGRITY of your CHARACTER. Remember, to be TRUSTED is a "blessing"...BE someone that can be TRUSTED ♥ CREDENCE in another is one of the most important factors in SUSTAINING any relationship. When told something in SECRECY, keep your UPRIGHT "standing" by not "spilling" the "beans"! Provide a "soft place to land" by being the person that others feel "comfortable" CONFIDING in. Do not take on the added role of a "GOSSIP columnist"...the words that "compose" your PUBLIC "newsfeeds" should never involve another's PRIVATE details ♥ The "WEALTH" of RELIANCE takes a long time to EARN, but only a second to "BANKRUPT" if "spent" foolishly. "Unlock" your "VAULT" for one to SECURE their VALUABLE information in, but then throw away the "KEY"! The EARNED trust of another is one of your greatest ASSETS ♥ (LCF)

WAKE UP AND PAY ATTENTION

♥ As you go about your day, be ATTENTIVE to your tasks "AT HAND" in order to stay "ON YOUR TOES"! ♥ Stay in the "CURRENT" moment to prevent yourself from "DRIFTING" away in a DAYDREAM. Avoid getting "SINGLED" out for underperformance by being fully "ENGAGED" in your daily actions...and INTERactions. BE PRESENT in another's presence ♥ "HANG ON" every word that is spoken to you so that your attention doesn't "SLIP"...when you are "ALL EARS", you are the type of company that ENDEARS...By staying "AWARE", it shows that you CARE. Earn the "INTEREST" of others by staying "INVESTED" in their "COMPANY" ♥ Put yourself on high "ALERT", "WAKE UP" and pay attention to life! To give your best EFFORT, stay "ON THE BALL" and always give your "ALL"! ♥ (LCF)

WALK IN FAITH

♥ If you ever get "DOWN" to the point where you feel like there is no HOPE, you must TRUST that the only "direction" from where you are is "UP". "Hold on" to an "attitude" of "CERTITUDE" and "let go" of any "DISSENSION" in order to start your "ASCENTION" ♥ While it can prove difficult to "SEE" at a time when you are "blinded" by the "BLUES", it is up to you to "CHOOSE" to keep your "eyes open WIDE" for the "BRIGHT SIDE" ♥ UNDERSTAND that God always has your HAND...Do not be "mistaken" in thinking that you will ever be "forsaken". A "MASTER" makes NO MISTAKES and therefore, has no need for a "pencil"...remember that your life was "drawn" according to the most "DIVINE" "stencil" ♥ If you feel "trapped" in a "maze" of MELANCHOLY, have "NO DOUBT" that you will find your "JOLLY" way "OUT" ♥ Do not commit an act of "TREASON" by "DISBELIEVIN'" the fact that ALL THINGS happens for a pre-determined "REASON"! ♥ If "WAVERING" has caused you to "lose your balance" with its "sway", use this time "on your knees" to recollect yourself and PRAY. "Dust off" any DISBELIEF, "STAND UP" with CONVICTION, and let your SKEPTICISM "subside", for you will be headed toward a "HAVEN" of "AMAZIN'" when you allow FAITH to "GUIDE" your "STRIDE" ♥ (LCF)

Lauren Christine Frahn

WARM UP YOUR COLD FEET

♥ If you want to achieve anything of NOTORIETY, you must work past your ANXIETY ♥ Do not allow "ruminations" of TREPIDATION to cause your success's STAGNATION...Remove these thoughts of "DISMAY" and GET OUT OF YOUR OWN WAY! ♥ If you are holding "TIGHT" to feelings of "FRIGHT", it is time to release these "BUTTERFLIES" and allow them to take "FLIGHT" ♥ You cannot get working on your AMBITION's "INCEPTION" unless you move past your fear of "REJECTION". Remember, an initial "THUMBS DOWN" only serves as a "HELPING HAND", for a "rejection" ultimately serves to "POINT YOU" in the right "DIRECTION"! ♥ Even if you are initially given the "COLD SHOULDER", you are only steps away from the point where your DREAMS will "SMOLDER". "Warm up" your "COLD FEET" with the "FIRE" of your PASSION! ♥ Get past any "AGITATION" to arrive at your goal's "GLORIFICATION"...and let the only "PALPITATION" be from the cause of "CELEBRATION"! ♥ When "challenged" by WORRY, never back down in a "hurry", but look this "FEAR" in the face with a confident "STARE"... and always take the "DARE" ♥ (LCF)

WAVE YOUR THANK-YOU WAND

♥ Never underestimate the enormous POWER of PRAISE...When you give GRATITUDE a "try", you will see your BLESSINGS start to "MULTIPLY" ♥ You do not have to search very "far" to see just how BLESSED you ARE...Take a look "around" and notice the FORTUNES that "abound" ♥ "Elevate" your SPIRITS by "BOWING DOWN" to "everyday" RICHES...and ENRICH your days ♥ Offer THANKSGIVING for your WELL-BEING, for there is no greater WEALTH than that of your HEALTH ♥ Fill your HEART by giving LOVE to your FAMILY & FRIENDS...HAPPINESS will surround you by "SMILING ON" those around you ♥ Put yourself in a higher MOOD by giving thanks for your FOOD ♥ Give THANKS to "running WATER"...and "Replenish" an "arid" OUTLOOK in a "hurry" ♥ "Paint" yourself an amazing reality by RECOGNIZING the "masterpiece" of NATURE itself ♥ Show "COURTESY" for ELECTRICITY...and "light up" your spirits ♥ INCREASE your cash flow by "APPRECIATING" your MONEY ♥ Reduce overall STRIFE by being genuinely GRATEFUL for LIFE ♥ Wave your "THANK YOU" wand infinitely and add measureless "MAGIC" to your FATE because nothing is "too small" for the effects that these "two little words" can CREATE...When you take nothing "FOR GRANTED", your life will become "ENCHANTED" ♥ (LCF)

Lauren Christine Frahn

WEAR ONLY ONE HAT

♥ Aim to PLEASE...YOURSELF ♥ Understand that trying to PLEASE everyone is a losing "battle"..."Surrender" to the fact that it is OKAY if you do not ♥ If you try to meet the VARIOUS needs, wants, and expectations of the MANY that you encounter, somewhere along the way, YOU will get "lost". Never sacrifice GRATIFYING yourself in pursuit of SATISFYING someone else ♥ The only thing that is AMUSING about trying to "amuse" everyone is all of the DIFFERENT "hats" that you attempt to wear AT ONCE...only wear the ONE that MATCHES the "outfit" of your TRUE COLORS! ♥ Forever follow the "LIGHT" of your heart's DELIGHT...and those that have a PLACE for YOU in theirs will ALWAYS be in your shadow ♥ (LCF)

WHATEVER IT TAKES

♥ In whatever you UNDERTAKE, make no MISTAKE that there is ALWAYS A WAY to ACHIEVE when you take action on what you BELIEVE...MAKE IT HAPPEN ♥ Do not cheat yourself out of ALL that you CAN and WANT to do...No matter WHO ♥ OPEN another door EVERY time that one is shut...No matter WHAT ♥ OVERCOME obstacles time and time again...No matter WHEN ♥ Seize every OPPORTUNITY with BELIEF and never despair...No matter WHERE ♥ Make sure that your EFFORTS never lack and always ENDOW...No matter HOW ♥ Discipline yourself to never SETTLE for less by always STRIVING for MORE...ASPIRE to find the way to climb HIGHER ♥ Even if you miss your TARGET or it is not in clear SIGHT, you must not give up your FIGHT...You will find your AIM as long as you keep your head IN the game. Do not ask WHY, but APPLY yourself and TRY ♥ No matter how HIGH the STAKES...Do WHATEVER IT TAKES ♥ (LCF)

Lauren Christine Frahn

209

WHY STORES HAVE CATALOGS

♥ Everyone has DIFFERENT looks and styles...This is why shops carry a VARIETY of brands!! ♥ While they may not COINCIDE with yours, you do not reserve the right to CRITICIZE, for there is not one style that is "wrong" versus "right" ♥ While you are certainly entitled to your PREFERENCE, you are not "afforded" the right to VOICE it as CRITICISM. One's APPEARANCE itself makes a STATEMENT, but does not require one from you if it is not a POSITIVE one. If you feel the need to pass JUDGMENT, stay out of that department! ♥ It is our "MIXED BAG" world that makes it so unique and AMAZING...ACCEPT others as they are and do not CONDEMN individuality, but COMMEND it...remember, this is WHY STORES HAVE CATALOGS! ♥ (LCF)

WINGS OF FORGIVENESS

♥ When you CARRY "hard" feelings against another, the only one who feels that WEIGHT is YOU ♥ Think about it...the person that you are "holding a GRUDGE" against cannot feel the BURDEN that YOU are carrying. Remove the grudge and instead, grant GOOD WILL, in order to GLIDE through life with a much "LIGHTER load" ~ Eliminate the BLAME and "RISE ABOVE" this RESENTMENT ♥ ABSOLVE another in order to "set YOURSELF free", for in granting absolution, you will absolutely ARISE to a HIGHER quality of life ♥ True MERCY does not require a "SORRY", for you may never get one. Decide to personally SOAR by granting PARDON to another, obtain your "WINGS of FORGIVENESS"...and FREE YOURSELF TO FLY ♥ (LCF)

Lauren Christine Frahn

"WOW" DAY

♥ Will over Won't ♥ With Over Without ♥ Wakeful over Weary ♥ Well-nourished Over Weak ♥ Wholehearted Over Wimpy ♥ Wieldy Over Wild ♥ Willful Over Wandering ♥ With-it Over Withdrawal ♥ Winged Over Wilted ♥ Well-endowed Over Withering ♥ Well-being Over Weeping ♥ Wishful Over Worried ♥ Wide-eyed Over Watery-eyed ♥ Watchful Over Worn-out ♥ Warmth Over Weapon ♥ Wealth Over Waste ♥ Well-off Over Write-off ♥ Well-spoken Over Whispered ♥ Well-wishes Over Wisecracks ♥ Whistle Over Whimper ♥ Warmhearted Over Wicked ♥ Wholesomeness Over Wrath ♥ Winsome Over Worrisome ♥ Wonderful Over Wrongful ♥ Welcome Our World, With Open-eyed Wonder ♥ Make it a "WOW" day! ♥ (LCF)

WRITE YOUR OWN DEFINITION

♥ YOU are the AUTHOR of the book of "Your Life" ~ Be sure that every "CHAPTER" is capable of being "published" ♥ As humans, we have the ability to THINK... Think only the very BEST of yourself and what you REPRESENT ♥ We have the ability to ACT...Act in a way that brings out the very BEST of your CHARACTER and NEVER CHANGE what you do in life that brings this about. What brings YOU your JOY and SUCCESS is completely INDEPENDENT of that which does in another's ♥ We have the ability to COMPROMISE...Never "compromise yourself" by CHANGING WHO YOU ARE in order to be "ACCEPTED" by another. Do not make "ALTERATIONS" in order to "FIT" into another person's life, but instead, make it a point to "OUTGROW" them ♥ Never allow ANOTHER to "DEFINE" you, for only YOU should "write" your DEFINITION...Use only the BEST of TERMS, "ON your terms" ♥ Be sure that your life "STORY" is an AUTObiography and not "written" with someone else's "PEN" ♥ (LCF)

Lauren Christine Frahn

"YOU CAN'T" FICTION

♥ While there are certain things that require A LOT of EFFORT in order to achieve them, NOTHING is impossible! If you believe otherwise, it is time to "EVICT" the voice in your brain that is whispering these FALSEHOODS..."VACATE" the voice that is LYING to you ♥ The amount of work may seem insurmountable...until you CHOOSE to SURMOUNT it! Remember that often it is the ASPIRATION which requires the most "PERSPIRATION" that is the most REWARDING and worth the "SWEAT equity" ♥ Manage to MUTE the MISSTATEMENTS in your mind that say, "you can't". SELF-MOTIVATE with positive "INFLECTION" and CURE the "INFECTION" of SELF-DECEPTION. Do not utter UNTRUTHS to yourself that you are UNABLE, for you are doing a DISSERVICE with this DISHONESTY ♥ "DICTION" that DENIES you what IS possible is merely "FICTION". If you hear stories that tell of "SHORTCOMINGS" that LIMIT your GROWTH, recognize them as "TALL TALES"...and RISE ABOVE THE "LIES"! ♥ (LCF)

YOUR FOOT, THEIR SHOE

♥ Oftentimes, it may be difficult to COMPREHEND the ACTIONS or REACTIONS of another, but that is usually because YOU do not take the time to CREATE the UNDERSTANDING ♥ Take a moment to recall a time when you were in a SIMILAR situation and remember the FEELINGS that YOU experienced ~ it becomes much easier to RELATE to many people that you may have otherwise "walked" quickly away from. "SLOW your STRIDE" and "SOFTEN your STANCE" toward others by demonstrating WARMTH and COMPASSION ♥ Instead of telling another to "SHOO!", first put "YOUR foot in THEIR shoe"...You will likely see that it has a FAMILIAR "FIT". If you see that they are about to "TRIP", create a SAFE PLACE for them to "FALL" ♥ REPLACE IGNORANCE WITH EMPATHY...and forever leave your "FOOTPRINT" on the HEARTS of many ♥ (LCF)

Lauren Christine Frahn

YOUR GOD-POTENTIAL

♥ When you BELIEVE in YOURSELF, you unlock the potential to DO anything you want, to BE anything that you desire...to ACHIEVE anything that you dream ♥ There is a POWER inside each and EVERY one of us to live lives of SUCCESS and of ABUNDANCE ~ What that involves is different to each individual, but the feeling of the desired outcome is exactly the same... it is one of total BLISS ♥ The key is to BELIEVE that you can make this happen for yourself, because you absolutely CAN ~ Remember that you have "God-potential"...which is LIMITLESS! ♥ Determine all of your strengths and combine them with your pas-sions and get going on the path to achieving your dreams ♥ You have everything inside of you to live an amazing life ~ BELIEVE...EMBARK...and MAKE YOUR MARK... ♥ (LCF)